Furniture Making

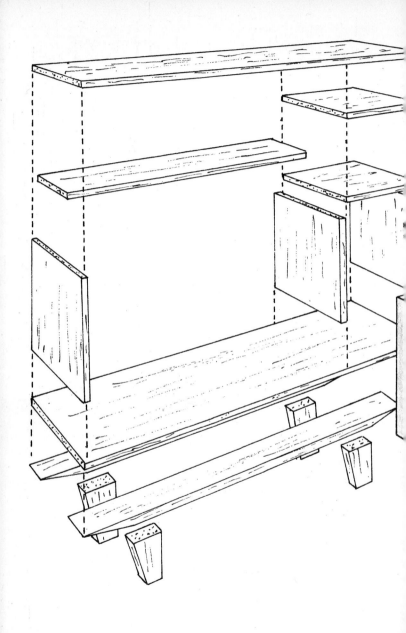

Furniture Making

David Collischon

Studio Vista London

Watson-Guptill Publications New York

For my Wife, Lesley

© David Collischon 1968
Published in London by Studio Vista Limited
Blue Star House, Highgate Hill, London N 19
and in New York by Watson-Guptill Publications
165 West 46th Street, New York 10036
Library of Congress Catalog Card Number 68-13122
Distributed in Canada by General Publishing Co. Ltd
30 Lesmill Road, Don Mills, Toronto, Canada
Set in Univers 8 and 9 pt.
by V. Siviter Smith & Co. Ltd, Birmingham
Printed in the Netherlands
by N.V. Grafische Industrie Haarlem

SBN 289 27862 7

Contents

Acknowledgments

The author wishes to thank Mr Bryan Smith of John Wright and Sons (Veneers) Ltd for his helpful comments on veneers and for the samples used in the illustration on page 87, also Stanley Works (G.B.) Ltd for the loan of many of the tools used in the illustrations.

Many thanks are also due to Penny Page for the hours she's spent typing and re-typing the manuscript and to her brother Clive for checking the technical details.

Introduction

Anyone can make their own furniture by the methods described in this book. There are no complicated woodwork joints because all the items are screwed and glued together and, when the construction is complete, each piece of furniture can be given the appearance of solid wood, by a very simple process of veneering. Accurate workmanship is, of course, essential but this is not difficult providing you take plenty of time. The results from veneering strong, well constructed items will be as pleasing and durable as solid wood—and a lot less expensive. Even if you have never handled a saw, screwdriver or any other tools, you will still be able to make all the items described and if you have already done some woodwork, then I hope in this book you will discover numerous ways of extending your hobby.

The first half of the book covers tools, how to use them and what materials to buy. It then describes at length one basic method of construction, showing how it can be adapted to cabinets, tables, chairs, drawers and practically every item of furniture. The second half deals with veneering.

You will, no doubt, have your own ideas about what you want to make, and so, instead of giving exact plans for every piece, I have treated them in general terms, showing how they are constructed but in most cases leaving the size, shape and appearance for you to decide. Throughout the book there are suggestions on how to adapt the designs and add special features, so that every item you make can be unique and tailored to your particular requirements.

I would advise you to read both parts of the book before starting; in this way you will get a better idea of the order in which things are done. Frequently it is easier to veneer sections during the construction, because they become inaccessible at later stages and therefore you need to know how to veneer almost as soon as you begin.

Terminology

It would be as well at the outset to define the terms and phrases which I have used, for although technical expressions have been avoided except where you might need to know them in order to purchase the right article, in explaining the construction, con-

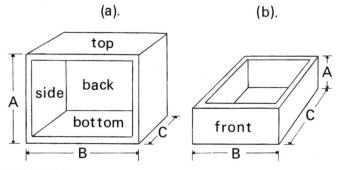

Fig. 2 A—height; B—width; C—depth

fusion can arise from such words as height and depth. The majority of the illustrations view the object from above and slightly to the side, thus you see the top, one side and front. Occasionally dotted lines show the other hidden dimensions if it helps to clarify the point. As you will see in fig. 2, the term 'width' refers to the measurement from side to side, 'depth' is front to back and 'height' top to bottom. Because of the thickness of timber (lumber in the United States) all measurements are given as either the internal or external dimension.

Various terms are used to describe a piece of wood or timber. A 'board' is any substantial length of solid, planed timber with surfaces at right angles, the width greater than the thickness. A 'block' is again a length of solid timber with the planed surfaces at right angles, but square or nearly square in section. In small sizes these are referred to as strips and unless I have specified otherwise, 'boards', 'blocks' and 'strips' should be taken as planed pine. The word 'sheet' covers plywood and other laminated or man-made timber bought by the square foot. Types and uses of timber are discussed in chapter 2.

1 The workshop and tools

The workshop

Woodwork inevitably causes a lot of dust and shavings, so it is not really practical to work in the house but neither is it necessary to have a large workshop. For years I worked in a narrow space, eight feet long by less than four feet wide, building everything in pieces and assembling them outside when the weather was fine.

The essential requirements are a firm level floor and a strong work bench. A garage or garden shed with a concrete floor is ideal, but if you have a concrete floor you will find it far less tiring if you make duckboards, as in fig. 4, on which to stand.

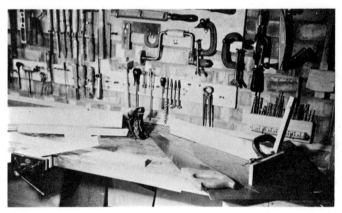

Fig. 3

The bench

This needs to be stoutly constructed with a top $1\frac{1}{2}$in. to 2in. thick. The size will be governed by the area of your 'workshop' but the larger the better, 4ft by 2ft being about the smallest practical working surface. A comfortable working height is about 30in. If you can get hold of an old kitchen or dining room table and suitably strengthen it, this is ideal, particularly if it has hinged flaps which can be raised to give the bench added length when required.

Fig. 4 is a suggested design for a home-made bench construct-ed on the 'rectangle' principle described in chapters 5 and 6. The legs are attached to the rectangle with four bolts and the top is constructed from boards screwed to the top of the rectangle over-lapping it two inches all round.

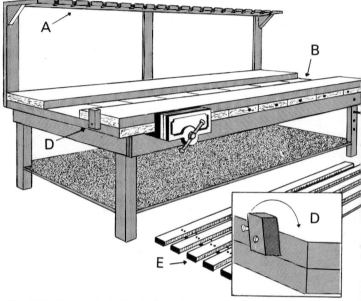

Fig. 4 Workbench. A—tool rack; B—tool trough; C—dowel peg for support-ing timber; D—end stop (also shown inset); E—duckboard

Two wider boards are then screwed at right angles leaving a trough in the centre for tools. When the bench is used for veneer-ing, a loose length of timber can be placed in the trough to make the bench level and a sheet of hardboard laid over the top to give a smooth cutting surface. The shelf is attached to the legs about six inches from the floor and end stops added at either side as shown in the inset diagram. The tool rack is optional, and if there is a wall nearby the alternative method shown in fig. 3, using spring clips and cup hooks, may be preferred, providing the work-shop is not damp or your tools will quickly go rusty.

Vice

Your woodwork vice, one with six-inch jaws will cover your requirements, should be permanently bolted to the bench so that the top of the jaw is level with the surface of the bench as in fig. 5. It may be necessary to add packing between the top of the fixing plate and the underside of the bench, and to drill large diameter holes in the 'rectangle' to take the rods on which the vice runs. The bolts holding the vice must be countersunk below the surface of the bench. Attach wooden blocks to both the jaws — you will find screw holes provided — as these will prevent damage to timber held in the vice. They should be the same size as the jaws and about $\frac{1}{4}$in. thick. The holes drilled in the leading edge of the bench and down the leg to the right of the vice (fig. 4) are for round pegs (dowels) to support the ends of lengths of timber held in the vice at varying angles.

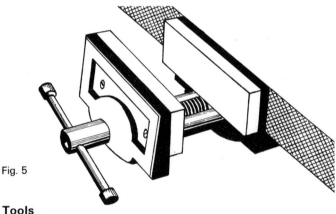

Fig. 5

Tools

Fig. 6 shows the tools which are required to tackle all the furniture covered in this book, although you will not use all of them for every item. I must emphasize that it pays to buy a reliable make such as 'Stanley' tools. A good tool will last a life time if it is well looked after; cheap ones will not only wear out quickly but also produce an inferior result.

Tools are roughly divided into four groups; measuring and marking; sawing, cutting and drilling; screwing and nailing;

11

clamping and holding. The following paragraph numbers correspond to the numbers in fig. 6.

1 12in. steel rule graduated in $\frac{1}{8}$ths, $\frac{1}{16}$ths and $\frac{1}{32}$nds. This is used for all fine measurements.

2 10ft pull-push rule with a locking device, graduated in $\frac{1}{16}$ths, which is used for measuring lengths of timber.

3 Carpenter's square with a 9in. blade—for testing the squareness of timber or a joint and for ruling at right angles to an edge.

4 Marking gauge, for scoring a line exactly parallel to an edge.

5 24in. cross cut saw for large pieces of timber.

6 14in. tenon saw for small timber, plywood and hardboard.

7 10in. keyhole saw for cutting centre shapes.

8 Trimming knife—numerous uses, including accurately marking out areas to be rebated (rabbeted in the United States).

9 $\frac{1}{4}$in., $\frac{1}{2}$in. firmer chisels and 1in. bevelled-edge chisel all of which are used for gouging and rebating.

10 8in. sweep brace, preferably rachet type.

11 $\frac{3}{8}$in., $\frac{1}{2}$in. and 1in. twist bits used in the brace for drilling dowel holes and starting holes for centre sawing.

12 $\frac{5}{16}$ths capacity hand drill.

13 $\frac{1}{16}$in., $\frac{3}{32}$in., $\frac{1}{8}$in., $\frac{5}{32}$in., $\frac{3}{16}$in. and $\frac{7}{32}$in. drill bits for drilling screw holes.

14 $\frac{3}{16}$in. and $\frac{1}{4}$in. masonry bits with tungsten carbide tips for drilling holes in walls.

15 9in. smooth plane with 2in. cutting blade.

16 10in. 'Surform' planer file for rounding edges and filing two adjacent surfaces level.

17 Hand held counter-sink bit for drilling a V shape to take screw heads. (Counter-sink bits can also be obtained for braces and hand drills.)

18 8in. blade ratchet screwdriver for normal steel screws.

19 6in. blade fixed screwdriver with fine point for small screws.

20 Bradawl used for starting holes for small screws and also for marking, through the hole drilled in one piece of timber, the point where the screw will bed in the piece behind.

21 Fine headed punch for tapping panel pins and veneer pins (fig. 14) beneath the surface.

22 10oz. plain face and pein hammer—the wide face for nails and the wedge face for panel and veneer pins.

23 8in. pincers for removing nails and panel pins.

24 5in. head wooden mallet for tapping chisels.

25 Four 3in. or 4in. G clamps (C clamps) for securing timber while it is being worked on.

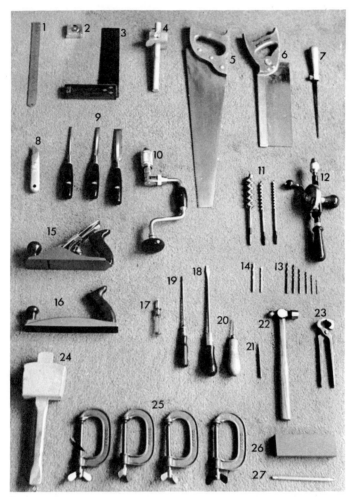

Fig. 6

26 8in. carborundum oilstone for sharpening chisels and the smooth plane.
27 Hard lead pencil – if you obtain a brightly coloured giant pencil it is easier to spot among shavings and other tools.

Fig. 7 a–h

14

Using the tools

Whilst it is fairly obvious how most of the tools work, the following brief notes and fig. 7 on their use will help you to obtain the best results, although, as you will appreciate whole books have been written on the use of tools alone.

Marking out timber. Place your pencil on the exact point at which the line is to be drawn and move the rule or square up to it. Fig. 7a shows the carpenter's square being used to test a right angle joint. For lines parallel to an edge, the marking gauge is set to the exact width either with a ruler or against the thickness of an item (fig. 7b) and used to score a line as in fig. 7c.

Sawing. The saw should be held so that the index finger points down the blade acting as a guide (fig. 7d). With the first few starting strokes use the thumb of the hand holding the timber to guide the side of the blade (fig. 7e). For testing the accuracy of a cut, mark the timber on all four surfaces; when you have sawn, there should be no trace of the pencil mark on either piece of timber. On the last few strokes, support the end of the timber to prevent its own weight causing it to splinter. When using the tenon saw to cut plywood, the cutting edge should be at an angle of about 15° to the surface so that the metal back of the saw clears the timber (fig. 7f). Always lightly rub off (sand down) the splinters after sawing.

Chiselling. Work with the timber secured in the vice or with G cramps (C clamps). If more than hand pressure is needed, tap the end of the handle with the mallet, although strictly this is bad practice with bevel-edged chisels. Both hands should always be behind the cutting surface, the bevelled edge of the blade upper-most and held almost parallel to the base of the rebate (rabbet) (fig. 7g). Do not insert the blade at the full depth of the portion to be removed, instead take a series of thin wafers, pulling down on the chisel handle to lever the chip out.

Trimming. Hold the knife with the index finger along the top and whenever possible cut against a steel rule. Draw the knife towards you, again making sure that your holding hand is behind the cutting edge.

Drilling. Let the drill draw itself into the timber. To drill to an exact depth, tie a piece of cotton round the bit at the depth required.

Planing. The plane will tend to remove a deeper shaving towards the end of its sweep, so pressure should be gradually eased from about half way along. Always plane with the grain (see page 18), the sole of the plane square to the surface (fig. 7h).

Countersinking. The V shaped gouge should be deep enough to bed the screw level with the surface of the timber.

Hammering. Hold the hammer at the end of the handle to get the maximum leverage and keep your eye on the head of the nail.

Screwing. As with a drill, a screw is designed so that it is drawn by its own thread into the timber; pressure should not be necessary if the holes have been correctly drilled (see page 19).

Care of tools

The tools which require sharpening are the chisels, smooth plane and saws. The saw is a skilled job and I suggest that it is professionally reset and sharpened. Chisels, however, need sharpening as soon as they are bought. This is done on the oilstone. The bevelled edge is laid practically flat on the stone as in fig. 8, and the blade moved up and down the full length of the stone. Finish with a few light strokes with the blade flat on its back to remove any slight burr. A whole chapter could be devoted to sharpening tools, and I strongly recommend further reading*. If you know someone who can demonstrate the correct methods, this is even better.

To prevent rust, the metal parts of tools should be wiped over with a light oily rag and the saw blades with linseed oil.

Fig. 8

There are numerous additional tools on the market and the more you progress the more you will want to explore the avenues opened up by tools designed to do different jobs.

Woodcarving for Beginners, Charles Graveney, Pocket How To Do It, Studio Vista Limited, London, Watson-Guptill Publications, New York.

2 Materials

Timber (Lumber)

Timber is classified into hardwoods which come from deciduous trees and softwoods which are obtained from coniferous varieties. It is misleading, however, to regard these classifications as descriptive of their properties as some softwoods are extremely hard and vice versa. Timber is sold either as 'sawn' ('rough-cut') or 'planed' ('dressed') and it is advisable always to purchase the latter as this saves the problem of planing to size. When designing furniture it is well worth checking on your local timber yard's 'stock' sizes, using these wherever possible.

Timber measurements are, however, quoted in sawn (rough-cut) sizes therefore if you ask for a board 1in. thick by 4in. wide you will receive one which is approximately $\frac{7}{8}$in. thick by $3\frac{7}{8}$in. wide, $\frac{1}{16}$in. or perhaps more having been removed from each surface in the planing. This does not apply in the case of sheets, which are normally sold to their true size.

Boards and blocks can normally be purchased by the foot (running foot) and sheets by the square foot, although, in the case of sheets, it is very much cheaper per square foot to buy a

Fig. 9

complete sheet. With strips and mouldings, some of which are shown in fig. 9, I find most timber yards expect one to buy the complete length.

Pine is the most suitable timber for amateur woodworking. It is available in a large range of planed (dressed) sizes from $\frac{1}{2}$in. to 2in. thick and up to 10in. or 12in. wide. It is easy to work and moderately priced, but care must be taken to select boards that are free from large knots. (In the United States three grades of pine are available. Top grade, called clear pine, is free of knots. Grade two common pine, has small tight knots, except at the edges which are generally clear. Grade three common pine can have large knots throughout, and is frequently referred to as shelving pine.) Parana and clear pine, although a little more expensive, are the best and most reliable varieties, ideally suitable for cabinets, frames, shelves and drawers.

For legs, edging, runners and thin partitions a rather harder variety of timber is preferable, such as ramin or poplar, which are available in smaller sizes than pine, although they are more expensive.

Plywood is suitable for covering large areas such as the backs of cabinets and drawer bottoms. It is available in sheets up to 4ft by 8ft or even larger to special order, and ranges in thickness from $\frac{1}{8}$in. upwards.

Blockboard or lumber core plywood (fig. 10) is also available in large sheets which range in thickness from $\frac{1}{2}$in. to 1in. This is best used for table tops and large firm areas where the use of boards would necessitate joining several widths.

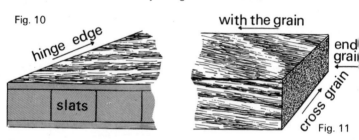

Fig. 10

with the grain

hinge edge

slats

end grain

cross grain

Fig. 11

A lot of detailed veneer edging work on cabinets and drawers can be avoided by leaving the interiors unveneered and, by selecting the timber carefully, you will be able to obtain a reasonable whiteish match between pine, ramin or poplar, plywood or blockboard, providing you avoid the reddish coloured gaboon-faced sheets or dark striped parana pine.

There are two further types of sheet, both man-made: chipboard and hardboard. Chipboard, as its name suggests, is compressed wood chips and requires veneering, and as a substitute for block-board, it is cheaper and almost as strong. (There is a brand of chipboard manufactured in the United States which is made especially for veneering. It goes by the name of Novaply Core Stock.) Hardboard (such as Masonite) can be substituted for plywood on the backs of cabinets but it will only take veneer on the smooth side.

The grain of timber seldom runs entirely parallel with the edge of the board or sheet, thus one says 'with the grain' or 'against the grain', and the direction of these is shown in fig. 11. If you are planing against the grain the cutting edge will tend to dig in and produce a rough finish. Sometimes two different directions of grain can be found on the same piece of timber. In this case it must be planed from different directions at the appropriate points. With blockboard (lumber core plywood) (fig. 10) the centre slats (core) are laid at right angles to the outer sheets, thus on doors and lids the outer grain should run at right angles to the hinges so that the screws are inserted in the side and not end grain of the slats.

Accessories

A small, basic stock of essential accessories eliminates the need for constant visits to the hardware store as each new stage in the construction is reached. If the right size screw is not to hand, there is always the temptation to 'make do' with the next best which invariably results either in weak construction or in splitting timber. It is less expensive to buy screws by the gross or half gross, and nails, which are bought by weight, are so cheap that it is worth buying three or four ounces of various sizes and types. Glasspaper (sandpaper) and glue are also needed at every stage of the construction. A suggested basic 'stock' list is given at the end of this chapter.

Fig. 12 Screws. A—countersunk (flat head); B—domed head (round head); C—raised head (oval head)

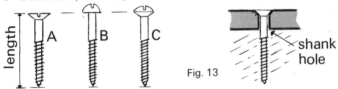

Fig. 13

Screws. There are three types of screw: countersunk (flat head), domed head (round head) and raised head (oval head). These are illustrated in fig. 12, which also shows how the length of a screw is measured. Screw thicknesses go by numbers, thus screws of different lengths but the same thickness are the same number. When a screw is used to join two pieces of timber, a hole of a slightly larger diameter than the shank of the screw should be drilled through the top piece as in fig. 13 and a start given to the

19

screw in the bottom piece of timber with the bradawl. The following table gives the size of the hand drill bit to use with the more common sizes of screw:

Bit	Screw No.	Bit	Screw No.
$\frac{3}{32}$	2	$\frac{3}{16}$	8
$\frac{1}{8}$	4	$\frac{7}{32}$	10
$\frac{5}{32}$	6	$\frac{1}{4}$	12

It is usually necessary to drill part of the hole in the second piece of timber. In such cases always use a drill at least one size thinner than that used for the shank hole, to make sure that the screw will bite, and only drill to half the depth to which the screw will bed.

Brass screws are preferable for the interiors of cabinets which are left unveneered. As these are rather more expensive, it is better to buy them as required, but take care not to exert undue pressure on a brass screw or it will snap.

Nails. There are several types of nails but the four which will be found most useful are shown in fig. 14. Veneer and panel pins (brads) are used for thin mouldings, plywood, or as a temporary holding measure. To prevent a nail from splitting thin wood, dull the point by tapping it with a hammer, this way it punches through the wood fibres instead of forcing them apart.

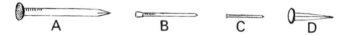

Fig. 14 Nails. A—wire nail; B—panel pin; C—veneer pin; D—tack

Glasspaper (Sandpaper). Although this goes by gauge it is sufficient simply to ask for coarse, medium or fine. For the final finish on veneer, flourpaper (garnet [7/0] paper) should be used. Coarse glasspaper (sandpaper) is very seldom used because it is very abrasive and will deeply score the surface. When preparing a surface which will remain visible, sand with the grain (see page 18), but if the surface is to be painted, sand across the grain. Even pressure on the surface can be achieved by wrapping the glasspaper round a wooden or cork block, folding the sheet in quarters.

Adhesives. There are so many varieties, with different methods of application now available, that it would be quite impossible to list them all. For general woodwork, either casein or resin glues are easy to use and do not require heating.

Screws (countersunk steel)
  1 gross ½in. No. 4
  ½ gross ¾in. No. 4
  1 gross 1in. No. 6
  1 gross 1in. No. 8
  ½ gross 1¼in. No. 8
  1 gross 1½in. No. 8
  ½ gross 2in. No. 8
Nails (fig. 14)
  4oz. 1in. wire
  4oz. 1½in. panel pins (brads)

4oz. 1in. panel pins
4oz. veneer pins
4oz. ¾in. tacks
Three sheets each of medium, fine glasspaper (sandpaper) and flourpaper (garnet paper)
One sheet of coarse glasspaper (sandpaper)
One ½lb tin of casein glue or resin glue and hardener.

3 Home-made equipment

One of the pleasures of carpentry is discovering or inventing gadgets which make the job simpler or easier. I cannot claim any originality for the three pieces of equipment in this chapter but in my workshop they are as essential and as much used as the manufactured tools. With the right timber all three can be made in less than an hour.

Bench hook

This is a tremendous help when sawing boards or blocks (fig. 15). You will need a 12in. board of 1in. × 6in. and a 9in. block of 1½in. × 1½in. Saw the block into two equal lengths; once each is

Fig. 15

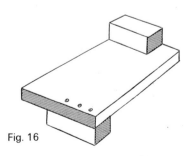

Fig. 16

firmly screwed and glued at opposite ends and on opposite sides of the board, as in fig. 16, your hook is ready for use. With this arrangement of the blocks, it doesn't matter whether you are right or left handed. I find it helps to have a second hook for sawing long pieces of timber as this keeps it parallel and therefore easier to cut accurately.

Right angle blocks and butt joints

Right angle blocks perform a vital function and, although they are simply a number of 2in. × 2in. hardwood blocks, of various lengths, in selecting the timber from which they are cut it is essential to go armed with your square. You must ensure that not only are all the surfaces exactly at right angles to each other (testing this down the whole of their length), but also that the block is completely warp free. To do this, lay the timber on a flat surface and draw a line along its full length. Rotate the timber to the next surface and check whether the second side is true with the pencil line. The most useful lengths for right angle blocks are 6in, 12in. and 24in., one of each.

The right angle joint is the key to successful furniture. It must be both accurate and strong but since, in this book, we are avoiding the more complicated woodwork joints, such as dove-tails, mortise and tenons and the like, the butt joints must be as near perfect as you can make them. A butt joint is simply two pieces of wood joined surface to surface without interlocking, held together by glue and screws. Therefore the first and most important feature is to ensure that the two surfaces are true and lie completely flush with each other. This means that accurate sawing is absolutely essential; but do not be daunted by this—it is only a matter of practice.

The butt joint can be made either in a T or an L shape. In both cases the two pieces of timber when viewed in cross section are at right angles.

We will look first at the T joint. At the point where the arm joins the cross member, using the square, draw a line across the width of the board, at right angles to the edge (fig. 17a). Draw a second line, allowing for the thickness of the arm, parallel with the first. These two lines mark the position of the butt joint. Midway between the two lines drill a series of equally spaced holes through the cross member, countersinking them on the side opposite the arm (fig. 17b). Next lay a right angle block exactly on one of the lines, clamping it to the cross member (fig. 17c). Position the G cramps (C clamps) so that their backs are against the right angle block well clear of the cross member. The butting surface of the arm is then glued, placed on the cross member against the block and held in position by two further G cramps

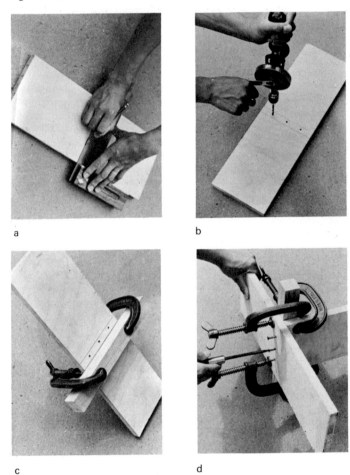

a

b

c

d

Fig. 17 a–d

(fig. 17d). Make sure that none of the glue gets onto the block or you will find this has also become part of your joint! With the two boards firmly in position, the screws can be inserted from the underside.

The L joint is made in exactly the same way. Mark the thickness of the arm on the end of the cross member, using the marking gauge (fig. 18a) and between this line and the end of the board drill the holes. The right angle block is clamped to the cross member (fig. 18b), followed by the upright (fig. 18c), which is then glued and screwed in position.

Whenever you join two pieces of timber at right angles, with screws, it is always safer to sight your holes at the point where they emerge on the underside of the top piece, to ensure that they are in the centre of the thickness of the second piece.

Although the explanation of this method of jointing is somewhat lengthy, it is in fact very quick and simple and you will rapidly become accustomed to marking the timber and attaching the G cramps. I often find that the position of the cramps has to be juggled slightly, depending on the thickness of the timber, but on small joints it is sufficient to use only one cramp in each direction.

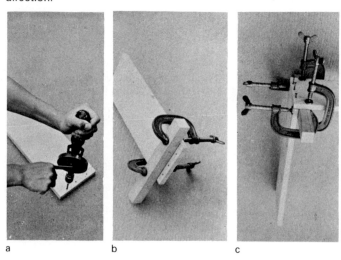

a   b   c

Fig. 18 a–c

This same jointing principle can be used where a diagonal butt joint is required. The only difference is in the position of the right angle block which is clamped diagonally across the board instead of at right angles to the edge (fig. 19).

Fig. 19

Rough rule and square test

This is two tools in·one. You require a 6ft, warp free strip of hardwood, $\frac{1}{2}$in. × $\frac{1}{2}$in. On one side mark off exact foot measurements scoring these with a shallow saw nick, cutting the timber to an exact five or six foot length. This provides a rough ruler which I find useful when sorting through timber to find pieces of roughly equal length. It also frequently proves useful as a straight edge for ruling lines linking two widely spaced points. On the opposite side, one inch from the end and in the centre of the strip, knock in a panel pin, leaving the head about $\frac{1}{4}$in. above the surface. This

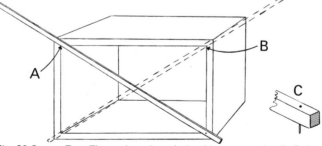

Fig. 20 Square Test. The mark made at A should correspond at B. C shows the veneer pin in the end of the rough rule

is used as in fig. 20, to test that a rectangular cabinet has right angle corners. The end with the panel pin is put in one corner and a pencil mark made on the rule where it dissects the corner diagonally opposite. The rule is then placed in the opposite corners and if the cabinet has right angled corners the mark will correspond. This is a more accurate test than the carpenter's square.

4
Getting
started

Fig. 21

Before we look at cabinets, chairs, drawers and all the larger pieces of furniture, you may like to practise on some small items, to get the feel of your tools, the timber and veneer. The three pieces in this chapter incorporate a number of features which occur in designs discussed later in the book, but they require only modest materials and can all be made in a few evenings.

Table lamp

Table lamps are particularly pleasing if their design is slightly unusual. Fig. 21, described in the following paragraphs, shows a lamp standing about 18in. high, complete with the shade. The size of the stand can, of course, be adjusted in proportion to the shade you wish to use. The materials are negligible, simply a 36in. board of 1in. × 3in. and a piece of $\frac{1}{8}$in. plywood, 9in. × 9in.

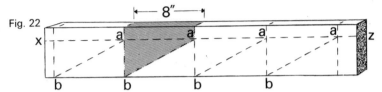

Fig. 22

For the base, measure the board into four 8in. lengths and at each point, using the square, draw a line round all four sides (fig. 22). On the wide side, with the marking gauge, score another line, x–z, the full length of the board, ¾in. from the edge. From the points where x–z crosses the right angle lines draw all the diagonals a–b. The four segments of the base are sawn at right angles then diagonally, to produce shapes like the one which is shaded.

You will find it easier if you start by sawing the right angle offcut at the right hand end, then clamp the timber so that the segment overhangs the end of the bench while you cut the diagonal, and so alternately down its length. Decide whether you would like the edges left square or rounded. If rounded, place each segment separately in the vice, the diagonally cut edge uppermost and parallel with the floor, and obtain the shape with the 'Surform' plane, remembering to plane with the grain. When the four pieces are stood up on their wide ends with the edges just touching they form a cross with a hollow square in the centre to take the flex (the lamp cord or wire), fig. 23.

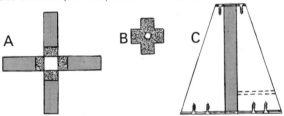

Fig. 23 A–plywood base; B–plywood top; C–cross section showing position of screws and hole for flex

Stand them on the plywood, and having made sure they are at right angles, draw round their outline, then cut the plywood cross with the keyhole saw. Put two ¾in. no. 4 screws through the plywood into the base of each segment, then turn the stand the right way up and do the same for the top, using just one screw in each segment.

For the flex, drill a $\frac{3}{8}$in. diameter hole in the centre of the top plywood cross and a $\frac{1}{4}$in. diameter hole through the middle of one segment, about 1in. from the bottom. Sand the plywood to the same contour as the segments and the lampstand is ready for veneering.

A special plastic or brass fitting with a threaded collar is screwed to the top of the base for the lamp holder; your local electrical shop can provide both these fittings. To finish off the base, and indeed any item which stands on furniture, it is useful to stick a piece of felt or thin rubber on the bottom to prevent scratching the surface.

Fig. 24 (Photo courtesy David Knowles)

Suspended wall shelf

Everyone will want to know how this stays up because it appears to have no visible means of support. Like all good ideas it is wonderfully simple, and can be used for many items that fit flush on a wall.

The shelf can again be more or less any size, the one shown in fig. 24 measures 3ft wide by 7in. deep. Assuming yours is the same, you will require a 4ft 6in. length of 1in. × 7in. board, and two steel 'escutcheon' or keyhole plates (fig. 25).

Saw the shelf to the length you want. It will improve the appearance if the front underside is planed to about half its thickness as in fig. 26. When you do this, draw straight lines on the underside and leading edge, planing up to them to ensure that you get a sharp outline at each of the angles.

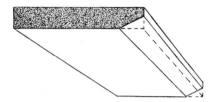

Fig. 25   Fig. 26

The end pieces can be any shape provided the back edge is flush to the wall and extends at least 4in. beneath the underside of the shelf, as it performs a vital weight-bearing function. The escutcheon plates—they must be the cast metal type, not plastic or tin as are sometimes sold—are fitted upside down, rebated (rabbeted) into the back of the end pieces, both exactly ½in. from the top (fig. 27). The best way of doing this is to hold the end

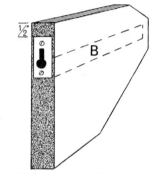

Fig. 27 Position of shelf shown by dotted lines round B

pieces in the vice and lay the plates in position, drawing round their outline with a knife, and at the same time making a cut the thickness of the plate. The rebate (rabbet) can then be gently removed with the ½in. firmer chisel. Before screwing the plate in position, trace round the keyhole outline, and with a ⅜in. bit, drill out two or three overlapping holes about ¼in. deep, behind the keyhole itself. The whole of the shelf section and the insides of the side pieces should then be veneered. The next operation, attaching the end pieces at right angles to the shelf, makes use of the right angle blocks and G cramps (C clamps) described in chapter 2. First draw two parallel lines on the insides of the end pieces, at right angles to their back edges, to mark the thickness of the shelf where it butts onto them. Midway between these two drill four $\frac{3}{16}$in. diameter holes about 1in. apart, countersinking them on the outside. Clamp a right angle block to the end piece, against the line marking the position of the underside of the shelf, then clamp the shelf to the block's upper surface as was shown in fig. 17d. Make sure that the back of the endpiece and the back of the shelf are flush with each other. The screws, 2in. no. 8s, can then be put in from the outside, and when both end pieces are in place the shelf is complete, apart from the remaining pieces of veneer.

To hang the shelf, measure the distance between the centres of the slots in the escutcheon plates and put two dome head (round head) screws into the wall, leaving their shanks proud by the thickness of the escutcheon plates. The dome heads (round heads) then fit through the holes in the plates and are held at the top end of the slots.

Fig. 28

Occasional tables

Bedside tables, coffee tables, television tables, telephone tables, it is surprising the number of little tables the average household needs and if you are one short, the design described in the next few paragraphs will provide a quick and attractive solution. In many ways it is the simplest of the three items in this chapter, but it will give you most scope for designing in veneer.

The table in fig. 28 stands 17in. high and has a top 30in. by 18in.

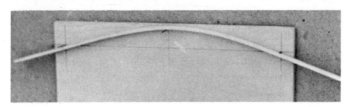

Fig. 29

For one of similar size you will require a sheet of ½in. chipboard 30in. × 18in., a 5ft board of 1in. × 3in., a set of pre-shaped legs 15in. long and two strips of ¼in. × ½in. hardwood.

You can make the table more interesting by curving the sides, ends or both, and for this you will need a template, produced by arranging three panel pins or brads on the chipboard as in fig. 29, with the hardwood strips 'sprung' round them. The shape produced by the strips is drawn onto the chipboard at both ends, taking care to get the panel pins (brads) in the same relative positions—the sharpness of the curve can be adjusted by altering their position up or down as required. Cut the outline with the keyhole saw, making sure that you keep the blade at right angles to the surface.

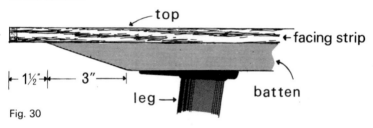

Fig. 30

The edges of the table top will have to be faced with the ¼in. × ½in. strips. Cut them into pieces about ½in. longer than each edge and drill ⅛in. holes down the centre of their wide sides, at roughly four-inch intervals; making sure there is a hole within an inch of all the ends. Having countersunk them, glue and screw them to the sides using ¾in. no. 4 screws and then trim them exactly to length. If you decide to give your table curved ends, the ends of the edging strips must follow the same contours. You will find it much easier to cut this shape correctly with the strips screwed in place. On the curved edges it is best to put one screw in the middle of the strip and then work out to each end.

Next two battens (boards) must be fitted to the underside to take the legs. Cut from the 1in. × 3in. board, they should be 3in. shorter than the length of the table top, their thickness tapered for three inches at either end (fig. 30). They are fixed to the underside of the table 1½in. from the sides and ends, with 1¼in. no. 8 screws, and the metal plates for the legs are screwed onto them, as shown in fig. 30, after veneering. A fuller description of pre-shaped legs is given in chapter 6.

Making the three items in this chapter has involved practically all the tools suggested for your workshop. In the next part of the book we shall be looking at larger and more involved pieces of furniture but do not be put off by this. I have often found the larger the item, the easier it is to construct.

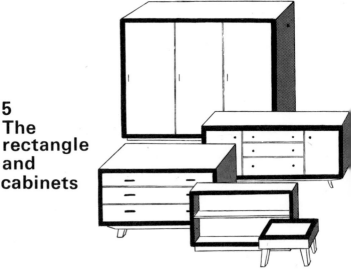

5
The
rectangle
and
cabinets

If you examine large pieces of furniture, such as cupboards, dressing tables, bookcases or wardrobes, you will notice that they nearly all have a common shape—the rectangle.

With upright furniture, the rectangle is usually their own outline formed by the top, bottom and side surfaces. Some pieces of furniture are made up of several separate rectangles. In a chest of drawers, for instance, each drawer is a rectangle on its back within the larger rectangle of the frame. The illustration on the front cover of this book is also an example of many rectangles making up the one piece of furniture. Chairs, tables and stools have a horizontal rectangle with the legs extending beneath and the seat or surface resting on top.

In the same way that a house gains both its shape and strength from the foundations, a piece of furniture needs a firm framework onto which other parts can be added. In the majority of cases this basic shape, the rectangle, can be made quite simply from four pieces of timber. This does not mean that the shape of the finished item will necessarily be rectangular, nor does it mean that the four pieces have to be of uniform depth or thickness. But because it is a rectangle, the internal dimensions of opposite surfaces must be the same length.

In manufactured furniture, the surfaces forming the rectangle are often made of a framework sheeted in with plywood. All the designs in this book show the rectangle constructed from solid timber, since it is easier to assemble and will produce a stronger result. You will no doubt wish to adapt the designs but the rectangle is always a good starting point.

Why a rectangle and not a square? The only reason is that the rectangle usually creates a more interesting shape either upright or horizontally.

Because the ultimate success of your furniture depends on the accuracy of the rectangle, it is worth spending some time over its construction. If the corners are not right angles, backs, doors and shelves will all have to be cut off-square, and nothing is more complicated than trying to hang doors on a framework which is out of line. In fact it is almost impossible.

In this chapter, to avoid confusion, I shall only refer to dimensions and thicknesses when it is necessary to give an indication of the size or strength of timber for various parts. The principles of

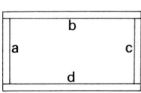
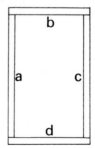

Fig. 32

Fig. 33 Bookcases, oak veneer on pine

Fig. 34 Coffee table, teak veneer on pine with vitreous glass mosaic top

construction apply whatever the size of the furniture, the size of the timber, or shape of the rectangle. In chapter 9, which deals with design, there are a number of plans on which to base your own designs and from these you will see what thickness of timber is recommended in relation to the overall size of the furniture.

Constructing the rectangle

Imagine that fig. 32 represents the front view of two cabinets, one long and low, the other tall and narrow. You will see that in both diagrams, the pieces a and c fit between b and d. Thus d, the base, supports the weight of everything above it. You must first decide on the width of the base, then cut two pieces of timber, the top and bottom, to exactly this width from either boards or sheet. You may decide that for a heavy item the base, d, needs to be thicker than top.

Next, the sides: as these will fit between the top and bottom pieces, their height will be the external height of the furniture, less the thickness of the top and bottom. In determining the height of the sides, you must also take into account the height of the legs or base you intend using.

Once you have cut all four pieces of timber, and checked that the pieces opposite each other are the same length, you will probably find it easier to veneer the inside surfaces before

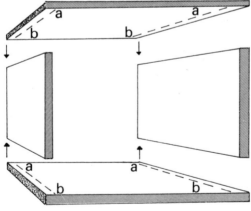

Fig. 35

assembling them. To put the rectangle together, using the marking guage, mark on the inside of the top and bottom pieces, at each end, the four lines a−b (fig. 35) representing the thicknesses of the side pieces. Between these lines and the ends of the timber, drill a series of holes, regularly spaced, countersinking them on the external sides. Then, using the right angle blocks and G cramps (C clamps) (as described in chapter 3), join all four pieces together with glue and screws which bed well into the sides of the rectangle. When completed, check the accuracy of the rectangle with the square test (also described in chapter 3).

Enclosing the rectangle

Having completed the basic rectangle, now let us look at its next stage of development.

If it is to be a cabinet it will need a back of plywood or $\frac{1}{8}$in. hardboard. Lay the frame over the sheet and draw round both the outside and inside, then, having removed the frame, cut the sheet round the outer line with the tenon saw. Midway between the edge and the inner pencil lines, mark at fairly close regular intervals the points for the screws (fig. 36), drilling and counter-

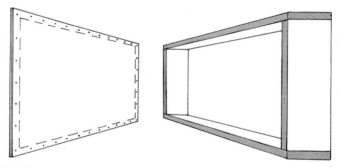

Fig. 36

sinking the holes at the back of the sheet. It is again much easier to veneer and rub down the sheet before putting it onto the rectangle. Glue the edges and then lay it on the rectangle and screw it down. I find that a veneer pin at each corner helps to keep it in place while the screws are put in. Finally, to complete the enclosed rectangle, the edges of the sheet will probably need

Fig. 37

filing flush with the sides. This can be done with the Surform file, but plane across the edge onto the sides (fig. 37) or you may rip the edge of the sheet. Putting a back on, even though it is only thin plywood held with short screws, adds considerably to the strength and rigidity of the rectangle.

Inserting fixed shelves

In addition to the timber for the shelves, you will need $\frac{1}{2}$in. × $\frac{1}{2}$in. strips of hardwood on which to support them at the sides. If you would like several shelves at varying heights, it is better to make the wider gaps at the bottom, otherwise the cabinet will look rather top heavy. Measure the position of the top surface of each shelf (fig. 38) and draw a horizontal line at this point on the inside of both sides of the rectangle and along the back. Allowing for the thickness of the shelf, rule a second line beneath the first, then drill a series of holes in the centre of the lines. The holes in the sides will need to take larger screws than the ones along the back.

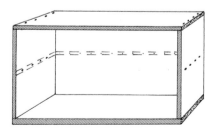

Fig. 38

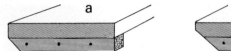
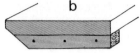

Fig. 39

The front edges of the $\frac{1}{2}$in. × $\frac{1}{2}$in. hardwood strips which support the shelves should be bevelled as in figs. 39a or b; their length depends upon the shape of the underside of the shelf. Drill about three holes in the sides of the strips, screwing and glueing them to the sides of the rectangle so that their top surfaces are flush with the line marking the underside of the shelf. Cut the shelves exactly to length, aiming at a tight fit without forcing the sides of the rectangle apart, veneer their top, bottom and front surfaces and screw them in position from the outside making sure they are flush with the back. They need a dab of glue wherever they come in contact with the rectangle and back but be careful not to put too much on or it will be squeezed out and may stain the veneer.

Shelves up to 30in. wide, 6in. deep can be made from good quality pine but if they are to be wider than this, 1in. blockboard would be more suitable, with the slats running the width.

Partitions and dividers

Beyond about 42in. in width and 10in. in depth, whatever material is used, the front edges of the shelves and the rectangle are almost certain to bow if they have any weight to bear. The only way to prevent this is to add partitions, which are, in effect, vertical shelves. They are measured off and fitted within the

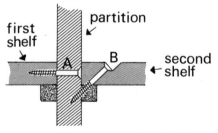

Fig. 40 The screws at A are inserted first and care needs to be taken over the length and positioning of the ones at B

rectangle in exactly the same way as shelves, except that they do not require the supporting blocks. They should be veneered, and attached after the back is added but before any of the shelves are put in. Shelves are fitted to the partitions, as though it were the side of the rectangle. If they run either side of the partition at exactly the same level they have to be attached to it with diagonal screws, as in fig. 40. This means that the top of the shelf must be left unveneered until it is screwed in position and the screw heads filled.

One of the advantages of making your own furniture is that it can be tailored to fit the items you intend to put in it. Space can be saved in a bookcase which has to accommodate several different heights of book, by fitting the shelves at various levels (fig. 41). In a wardrobe divided by one central partition (fig. 42), one side could be fitted with shelves, the other left empty as a full length hanging space.

Fig. 41

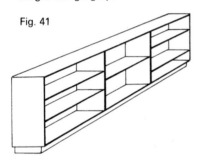

Fig. 42

Thin partitions which have no weight bearing function, or dividers as I prefer to call them, are extremely useful for keeping items separated, as for example in a cutlery drawer (fig. 43) or a cabinet for gramophone (phonograph) records (fig. 44).

Because they are plywood or $\frac{1}{4}$in. thick hardwood, they have to be attached to the rectangle with veneer and panel pins (brads) rather than screws. Mark the positions of the dividers on the inside of the rectangle, in the same way as for shelves, but drill only $\frac{1}{16}$in. diameter holes between the lines. Glue the edges of the dividers and through the sides, top and bottom of the rectangle use panel pins (brads) about $\frac{1}{4}$in. longer than the thickness of the timber, just enough to catch the edges of the dividers. At the back, through the sheeting, use $\frac{1}{2}$in. veneer pins. The glue does

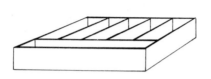

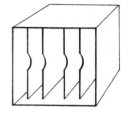

Fig. 43   Fig. 44

most of the holding. You will find that having pre-drilled the holes for the pins, there is no danger of their coming through at the wrong point and splitting the very thin edge of the divider. If you join dividers at right angles to each other within the drawer, pre-drill the holes at the butt joint, and again use veneer pins instead of panel pins.

Fig. 45 Flush-fitting drawers

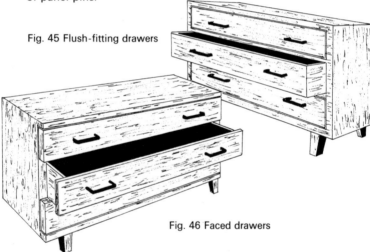

Fig. 46 Faced drawers

Drawers

The secret of a successful drawer is to leave just sufficient space between the side of the cabinet and the side of the drawer to allow for easy movement but not enough for it to become crooked and jam. A cabinet can have any number of drawers, but first decide whether you prefer flush fitting drawers (fig. 45) or faced drawers (fig. 46).

If you are making a unit with several drawers, whilst their heights can vary, their widths and depths must be identical and, for reasons of strength, the back and front sections of each drawer are screwed between the sides as in fig. 47. I find it best to cut all the sections out before assembling any of them, as in this way it is easier to check that they are all the same.

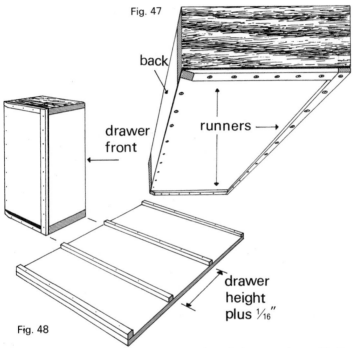

Fig. 47

back

drawer front

runners →

drawer height plus $\frac{1}{16}$"

Fig. 48

Having made the drawers, complete their veneering with the exception of the fronts. On the underneath, along the sides and front of the drawer screw $\frac{1}{4}$in. × $\frac{1}{2}$in. hardwood runners (fig. 47), flush with the edges, making sure that the screws are well countersunk.

Cut the sides of the cabinet from blockboard, to the same depth as the drawers but do not at this stage cut them to their exact height. Each drawer slides on $\frac{1}{2}$in. × $\frac{1}{2}$in. hardwood runners. Screw the bottom runner flush with the bottom edge of the cabinet

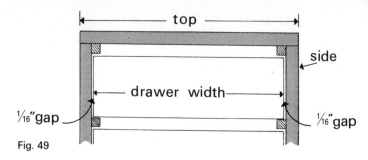

Fig. 49

side and the rest, which must be absolutely parallel to the bottom runner, are the full height of the drawer which will run between them *plus* $\frac{1}{16}$in. apart (fig. 48). It is best to screw and glue them down one at a time, marking off their positions from the one beneath. Before screwing down the top runner, mark the position of its top surface and saw the cabinet side along this line. Complete the runners for both the sides, and check, by laying them side by side, that they are identical.

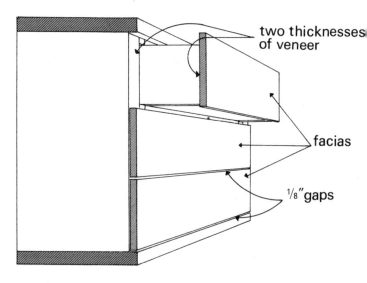

Fig. 50

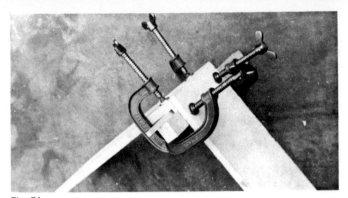

Fig. 51

The width of the top and bottom pieces of the cabinet rectangle are the width of the drawers, *plus* the thickness of the cabinet sides, *plus* an extra $\frac{1}{16}$in. either side for easy movement (fig. 49). Their depth, however, depends on how you intend to finish the drawer fronts. If these are to be flush with the cabinet sides as in fig. 45, the top and bottom of the cabinet rectangle will be the same depth as the sides. A more modern appearance is obtained by facing the drawers as in fig. 46. In this case the top and bottom must be wider, to allow not only for the thickness of the facing, which can be $\frac{1}{4}$in. plywood, but also for the thickness of veneer behind them and on the edge of the cabinet sides (fig. 50).

In putting the cabinet rectangle together, the runners on the sides create a slight problem, but this can be overcome by placing packing strips of $\frac{1}{2}$in. × $\frac{1}{2}$in. between the right angle blocks and the cabinet sides, as in fig. 51.

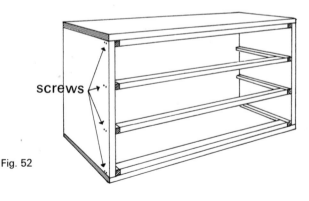

screws

Fig. 52

To strengthen the front of the cabinet, screw strips of $\frac{1}{2}$in. × 1in. at the front, between each of the runners (fig. 52). Make sure you cut them exactly to size, otherwise they will pull, or push, the cabinet out of shape.

Rub down all the surfaces which move and check that all the drawers fit well and run smoothly. Candle wax or soap smeared or rubbed on them will help to ensure that they do.

If the drawers fit flush with the sides, this completes the cabinet except for legs. If the drawers are to be faced, there should be a $\frac{1}{8}$in. gap between each facing (fig. 50). Their length should be the same as the external width of the cabinet. I find it best to cut all the facings out, lay the cabinet on its back with the drawers in place, then screw the facings on, checking that they are parallel with each other and lined up flush at each side of the cabinet.

6 Doors, hinges and legs

Almost every piece of furniture you make will require doors or legs, or both, and the rectangle figures largely in their construction. Doors can either be hinged or sliding. The latter are useful

Fig. 53 Teak veneered cabinet fitted with hardboard sliding doors

where space in front of the cabinet is limited; however, because one door has to pass in front of the other, it is difficult to use the cabinet or cupboard for items wider than the opening of one door. Hinged doors, on the other hand, do require very careful fitting.

Sliding doors

For most small cabinets plastic runners are ideal. The type which have slightly less than $\frac{1}{4}$in. wide channels should be used with doors cut from either $\frac{1}{8}$in. plywood or hardboard. Most hardware stores sell the runners in lengths ranging from 6 feet upwards, coloured either white or black. You will find that there are two heights of channel, the higher one being used at the top of the cabinet. One method of fitting the runners is to screw them inside the top and bottom of the cabinet, flush with the forward edges, as in the cross section diagram in fig. 54. This is not very satisfactory because not only is the overall height of the

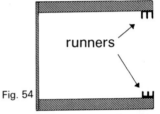

runners

Fig. 54

cabinet opening reduced by the height of the runners but also the lower runners create a lip over which items have to be lifted, instead of slid out. It is, therefore, better to drop the lower runner so that it is flush with the floor of the cabinet. As you will see from fig. 55 this can be done by mounting the runner on a thin packing strip so that the combined depth of the two is the same thickness as the base. This packing strip is attached to the base with 2in. no. 4 screws every few inches and also well glued. The runners need only tiny brass screws countersunk into the channels every few inches. The upper runner I do usually screw to the underside of the top but in order to make the top and bottom edges appear the same thickness, the timber for the bottom needs to be roughly double that of the top. By using 1in. chipboard or blockboard for the base and $\frac{1}{2}$in. for the top, the thicker base then provides sufficient edge on which to screw the packing strip.

The cabinet rectangle is built in the usual way, with the sides attached at right angles above the base, but the bottom edge of the sides must be cut to allow for the packing strips as can be seen in fig. 56. The rectangle should be completed and the runners attached before cutting the doors to size.

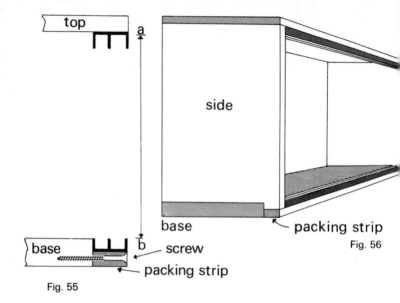

top

a

side

base

packing strip

Fig. 56

base   b   screw

packing strip

Fig. 55

The height of the doors is measured from the inside top of the upper channel, to the top edge of the corresponding lower channel measurement a–b (fig. 55). All the edges of the doors will, however, be veneered, so the height must take account of the thickness of veneer top and bottom. Their width is half the front internal measurement of the cabinet, plus about $\frac{1}{4}$in., to allow a slight overlap when both doors are closed. To retain the maximum effective opening, flush finger pulls are preferable to knobs or handles. The slight gap between the doors can be effectively sealed from dust by putting a strip of self adhesive foam draught excluder (weather stripping) behind the centre edge of the front door (fig. 57), or, alternatively, a strip of felt. Because

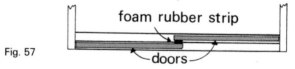

foam rubber strip

Fig. 57

doors

there is no tension or pull using impact adhesive (contact cement), it is unnecessary to veneer the reverse side of the doors

46

all over, but a 1in. frame round the back is advisable, to give the narrow edging strips adhesion, and also to fill out the channels. The veneer will stick easily to the faces of the runners on the front of the cabinet, but particular care needs to be taken over the unprotected edges to ensure a really good bond. The doors are fitted by inserting them in the top channel first and dropping them into the lower one; they will slide more easily if you rub soap or candle wax on all the moving parts.

For the heavier doors of wardrobes and large cupboards a rather more sophisticated type of sliding door tackle (hardware) must be used and there are numerous makes on the market. It is best to study them before building your furniture and to use hollow doors, which are described in the next section.

Hinged doors

Hinged doors can be made either from solid sheet or built up with a frame covered in $\frac{1}{8}$in. plywood or hardboard. For solid doors, blockboard (lumber core plywood) $\frac{1}{2}$in. or more thick, with slats running vertically, is the most suitable material as it will hold the hinge screws securely. If chipboard or plywoods are used they will require edging. Solid doors are very heavy and, if they are more than about four feet in height, inclined to whip or warp.

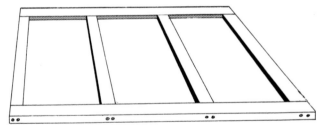

Fig. 58

Hollow doors, constructed on the rectangle principle (fig. 58), are therefore preferable. Choose timber with a $\frac{3}{4}$in. × $1\frac{1}{2}$in. section (or of similar proportions) for the frame, bearing in mind the additional thickness of the sheets either side, and build it up with cross members, using glue and two screws at each butt joint, and making sure that each corner is a right angle. Lay the frame on the sheet and draw round all the outlines, including the cross members. When you have done this on both the sheets, attach them to the frame, with your pencil marks on the outside surfaces. In this way you will know where the cross members are. The sheets are glued and screwed or nailed with veneer pins to the frame.

Fig. 59 (a) Doors mounted within the cabinet sides, (b) doors mounted on the face of the cabinet

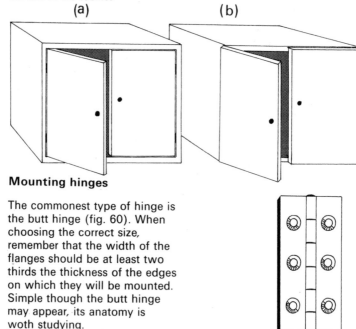

Mounting hinges

The commonest type of hinge is the butt hinge (fig. 60). When choosing the correct size, remember that the width of the flanges should be at least two thirds the thickness of the edges on which they will be mounted. Simple though the butt hinge may appear, its anatomy is woth studying.

The position of the hinges depends upon the type of doors you are fitting (as can be seen in fig. 61). Let us first consider doors set within the frame of the cabinet. In fig. 62, you will note that the flanges are parallel when the door is in the closed position, leaving a gap between the door and the frame. The size of the door should be smaller than the cabinet frame on all sides by the width of this gap, but also bear in mind, when cutting or constructing the door, that both it and the inside of the cabinet will be veneered and consequently the door must be these thicknesses smaller also, fractional though they are.

Fig. 60

48

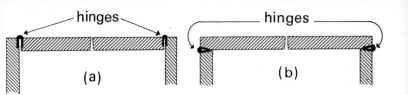

Fig. 61 Hinge positions viewed from above, (a) on doors fitted within the cabinet sides, (b) on doors fitted on the face of the cabinet

Having made the door to size, plane the open edge, as in fig. 63, to prevent it catching on the frame or the adjacent door; then veneer all the edges, as this makes the process of marking off the hinges much simpler.

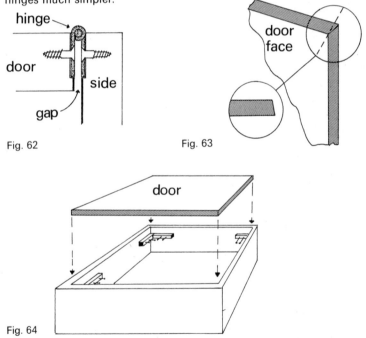

Fig. 62   Fig. 63

Fig. 64

When fitting the door you will have to devise a method of preventing it closing inwards. One way of doing this is to attach square strips to the frame on all four sides, against which the back of the door will rest when it is closed. If you decide to have only catches on the finished furniture, you will find it is a help to put temporary blocks inside the frame, the depth or thickness of the door, (fig. 64), whilst fitting the hinges. Lay the frame horizontally, resting the door on the blocks so that the gap is equal all round, and mark the top and bottom points of all the hinges, on both surfaces, to ensure that their positions correspond. Usually hinges are set at their own height from the top and bottom of the door; two are sufficient spaced at a maximum of 24in., but a third, in the centre, is necessary on longer edges.

Remove the door and complete the marking off for all the flanges as in fig. 65, a—a being the height of the hinge, a—b the measurement from the centre of the spindle to the edge of the flange and a—c the thickness of the flange.

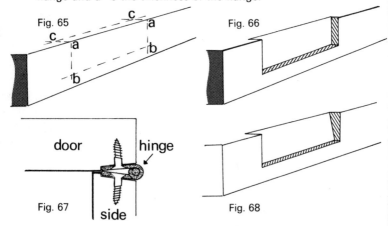

With the rebates (rabbets) cut, as in fig. 66, lay the door back on the blocks, check that the flanges all fit snugly opposite each other, then fit the centre screws only, testing that the door opens and closes easily leaving an equal gap all round. When all the veneering is completed, the other screws can be put in.

If your doors are designed to fit on the outside of the cabinet, all the hinge rebates (rabbets) will be wedge shaped, as in figs. 67 and 68. The doors should be the same size as the external dimensions of the cabinet and there should be no gap between the doors and the cabinet.

Fig. 69 Fireplace surround and shelf, teak veneer on pine and chipboard

Fig. 70 Cabinet, oak veneer on pine, chipboard and hardboard

Short legs and bases

You can introduce considerable variety by the use of a few basic designs for legs and bases. The simplest are blocks of wood, square or shaped, attached to battens (boards) and screwed to the underside of the cabinet as in fig. 71. This type of leg is most suitable for 'static' furniture, raising it only four or five inches above the floor. Its advantage lies in its simplicity.

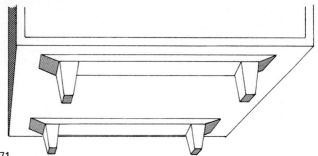

Fig. 71

An entirely different kind of base is the solid plinth, such as that used on the bookcases in fig. 33. This is a horizontal rectangle attached to the underside of the cabinet with right angle brackets (fig. 72). It is advisable to set it an inch or two behind the front of the cabinet to prevent it being scuffed with shoes. Although extremely rigid, and therefore particularly suitable for heavy items such as bookcases, it does look out of proportion if it is more than four or five inches high.

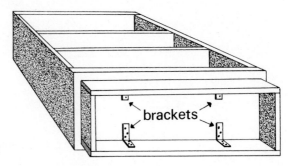

brackets

Fig. 72

There are on the market a number of ready-made legs which are very easily fitted (fig. 73). Each leg consists of a metal plate, which is attached to the underside of the cabinet or table, into which the leg screws. These are ideal for small items and, if you select either the square sided or round tapering designs, veneering them to match the rest of the cabinet presents no problems. They are available in lengths ranging from 6in. to 30in.

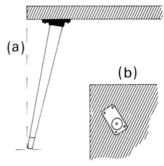

Fig. 73 (a) in cross section,
(b) position of plate

but the longer they are the less steady they become and even on light structures they tend to be rather unsatisfactory over about 18in.

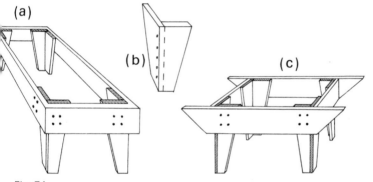

Fig. 74

For a rigid leg capable of bearing considerable weight it is necessary to construct both a rectangle frame and legs from boards (fig. 74a). The outer dimensions of the frame should be about 1in. smaller than the underside of the cabinet. Cut four identical legs from a 1in. thick board, tapering them towards the foot, on the sides facing inwards (fig. 74b). Glue and screw them firmly to the inside of the frame with their straight edges against the corners. A further four are then added at right angles to the

53

first, but, in order to maintain symmetry, their shape must be narrower by the thickness of the first four as shown by the dotted lines in fig. 74b. The second set, as well as being screwed and glued to the frame, are also screwed down their edge to the first four.

The whole frame can then be attached to the underside of the cabinet with right angle brackets in the same way as the solid base. This type of leg is very useful for stools; to give it more style, the long sides of the frame can be extended as in fig. 74c.

Table legs

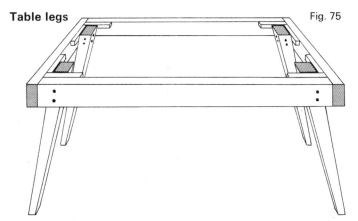

Fig. 75

Dining room tables, the surface of which should be about 28in. from the floor, require really strong steady legs. Again the rectangle forms the framework for both the top and the legs (fig. 75).

In a kitchen it is more practical to have a table with straight-edged vertical legs, but for a living room style is added by tapering and splaying the feet forwards and sideways.

For a table with a surface measuring 60in. × 30in., the frame can be made from 1in. × 5in. boards and the legs from $2\frac{1}{2}$in. × $2\frac{1}{2}$in. blocks, preferably hardwood. Cut the legs one inch longer than required, measuring them from the underside of the table top. Starting five inches from the top of each leg, taper them symmetrically with the plane to $1\frac{1}{4}$in. × $1\frac{1}{4}$in. at the foot. Ideally a jack plane, which is much longer than the smooth plane, should be used.

On the inside of the frame, at each corner flush with the top, screw two $\frac{3}{4}$in. × $\frac{3}{4}$in. hardwood blocks, about 3in. long, fig. 76.

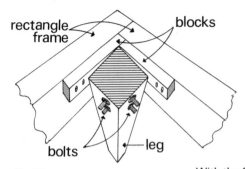

rectangle frame

blocks

bolts

leg

Fig. 76

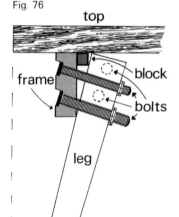

top

frame

block

bolts

leg

trim square

Fig. 77

With the G cramps (C clamps), fit each leg so that at the top it is held firmly against the corner formed by the blocks and at the bottom against the corner of the frame. The top of each leg should be flush with the top of the blocks. Through the sides of the frame and legs, drill two ¼in. diameter holes, 3in. apart so that they are at right angles to the slanting sides of the legs (fig. 77). The holes must be staggered to miss each other.

Attach the legs to the frame with 4in. × ¼in. diameter bolts, with two nuts on the inside to prevent them working loose. When fitting the bolts you will either have to countersink the heads or drill a large diameter hole to house them beneath the surface; these, of course, will have to be filled in before veneering.

When all the legs are firmly bolted in position, stand the frame and legs on a level surface and with a block of 1in. × 1in. go round the foot of each leg, using the block as a rule to

55

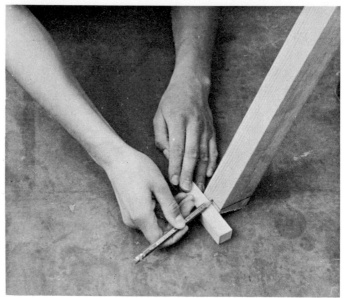

Fig. 78

mark a line parallel with the floor on each of its sides (fig. 78). Saw the legs off at this point, and the feet will rest square with the floor. This is not an easy saw cut because of the peculiar angles and it is best to saw down two of the surfaces at the same time so that you can watch two lines at once.

The measurements I have suggested for this type of leg will splay the foot of a 27in. leg approximately 3in. beyond the outer edges of the underside of the frame, therefore the table top needs to be at least this much larger all round. By increasing or reducing the size of the blocks at the top of the frame you can adjust the angle of the splay.

This method of bolting legs to the frame is much simpler if the legs are vertical. Blocks are not needed, and the legs are simply glued and bolted into the corner of the frame. In chapter 1, when describing the home-made bench, this method was suggested for the legs. You can be quite confident that, providing the timber is good, bolted legs will stand up to considerable weight and rough handling.

7
Easy chairs
divans
and
sofas

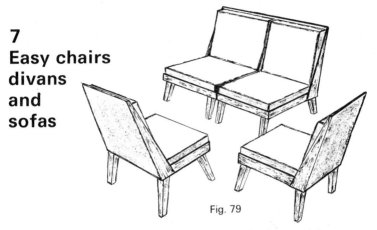

Fig. 79

The method suggested here for constructing the legs and frame for an easy chair is very similar to that used for the dining room table described in the last chapter, except that the legs are, of course, shorter, and the materials less substantial. To make a chair of reasonable proportions, the front of the seat should measure about 20in. and the sides between 22in. and 24in. The rectangle is constructed so that the front and back are screwed between the sides and it can be made from 1in. × 2½in. boards, with the legs from 1½in. × 1½in. hardwood blocks. Allowing for a three-inch high cushion on the seat, a comfortable height for the legs is about 12in., measured from the top of the rectangle. However, instead of splaying the legs diagonally, it is better simply to angle the front ones forward and the rear ones backward. Consequently only one block of hardwood is required at each corner

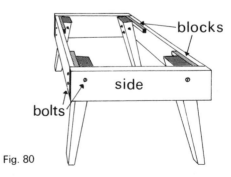

Fig. 80

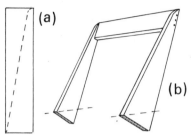

Fig. 81 (a) The dotted line indicates shape of upright, (b) the portion beneath the dotted lines is trimmed after attaching to the seat

(a)

(b)

of the frame, mounted on the front and back (fig. 80) and $\frac{1}{2}$in. × $\frac{1}{2}$in. will give the legs sufficient splay. Each leg is attached by the same method of bolting as used with the table, except that, since it is flush, it can be glued as well as bolted along the sides of the frame. At this stage, however, only put three $\frac{3}{16}$in. diameter 3in. bolts in each leg, leaving the lower one out on each side. The frame for the back consists of three pieces of timber, the two uprights which taper towards the top and a cross member. The uprights are cut from 1in. × 6in. boards and should be about 24in. high, tapering to about 1in. at the top. The cross member, from 1in. × 2$\frac{1}{2}$in., is screwed between these at the top so that its back is flush with the back of the uprights (fig. 81).

The length of the cross member should be the same as the external width of the seat.

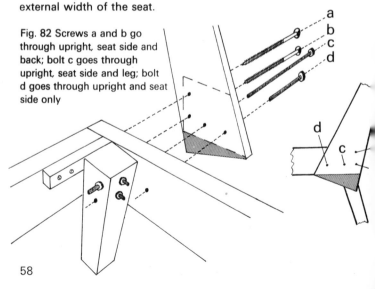

Fig. 82 Screws a and b go through upright, seat side and back; bolt c goes through upright, seat side and leg; bolt d goes through upright and seat side only

a
b
c
d

d

c

The uprights are attached at both sides of the seat rectangle with glue, two bolts and two screws (fig. 82). One 4in. bolt goes through the upright, the side of the frame and the leg. The second 2½in. bolt goes through the upright and the side of the frame only, forward of the leg. Both screws go through the uprights, and the ends of the sides and also penetrate the back timber of the rectangle frame, they therefore need to be 3in. no. 8s. When placing them, take care to avoid the screws already holding the rectangle together.

I find it easier to put the back on with the help of the G cramps (C clamps), getting the angle I want and then sawing the bottoms off the uprights (shaded areas in fig. 82), so that they are level with the underside of the seat. The angle of the back is entirely a matter of choice and will depend on the use to which the chair will be put. The seat can be made to slope down at the back by making the back legs shorter than the front. In the two profile views (figs. 83 a, b), the back is at the same angle to the seat but in b the back legs have been reduced in height.

Fig. 83

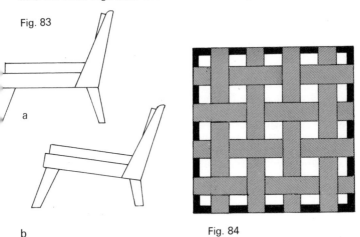

a

b

Fig. 84

There are two ways of filling in the seat. It can either be sheeted with ¼in. plywood on the top of the frame, or, to produce a softer effect, it can be webbed with 2in. wide nylon, laid criss-cross, as in fig. 84, and firmly tacked to the side. If you decide to use nylon, cut each strip of webbing to the right length and singe the ends

59

to stop them fraying. The back can simply be sheeted from top to bottom with $\frac{1}{4}$in. plywood screwed to the uprights, cross member and bottom of the rectangle frame. The chair is designed to take two covered foam rubber cushions, one laid on the seat and the other against the back so that it fits beneath the cross member and between the uprights as in fig. 79.

Fig. 85 Divan with headboard veneered in oak

Single divans (sofas)

In many ways the single divan is one of the simplest of all pieces of furniture to make. The horizontal rectangle must be made of sturdy timber, either $1\frac{1}{2}$in. × 10in. boards or 1in. blockboard (lumber core plywood). The rectangle is straightforward and it makes no difference whether you screw the sides within the ends or vice versa. Its outer dimensions will depend upon the size of the mattress you intend to use and the two should be the same area. Once the basic rectangle has been constructed, it will need a considerable amount of extra strengthening. At each of the inside corners glue and screw 2in. × 2in. blocks as in fig. 86, their tops $\frac{1}{2}$in. below the top of the rectangle. In the centre of the rectangle, also $\frac{1}{2}$in. below the top, screw and glue two cross members cut from 1in. × 3in. boards spacing them equidistant between each other and the ends. Level with the tops of the corner blocks and the cross members, screw and glue boards of $\frac{1}{2}$in. × 1in., with their wide edges along the sides, thereby forming a continuous ledge round the whole of the inside. Then fill in the top with $\frac{1}{4}$in. plywood.

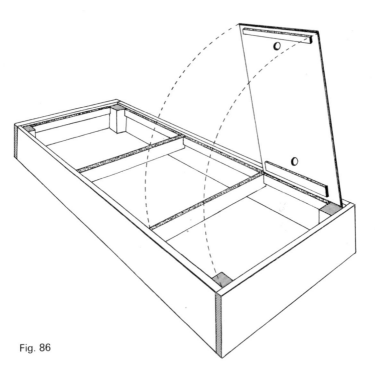

Fig. 86

Rather than waste all the space under this top you can make a huge drawer by sheeting in the bottom of the rectangle. This is made accessible by cutting the top sheeting into three pieces with the joints over the cross members. Drill a 1in. finger hole in each sheet, so that it can be lifted up independently and keep the sheets in position on the frame with small blocks fitted on their underside, as in fig. 86. The top edges of the rectangle are better if they are rounded on the outer side as they must, of course, be very smooth to prevent tearing the bed linen. Because divans are usually covered with a counterpane (slipcover) there is little point in veneering the sides; they can simply be painted. Alternatively you may wish to cover them in fabric.

A divan does not need legs but you will probably wish to add castors. Attach these to the bottom of the 2in. × 2in. blocks at each corner.

Double divans (sofas)

By comparing figs 87 and 86 you will see the main differences in the construction of a double divan. The two cross members extend to the bottom of the rectangle and are made of the same thickness of timber as the sides. A series of smaller staggered cross members from 1in. × 3in. boards are then screwed between the ends and each of the main cross members. Instead of four castors, six are used and the 2in. × 2in. blocks on which to support the extra pair are screwed half way along the sides. Three sheets of ¼in. plywood between each main cross member again provide the top.

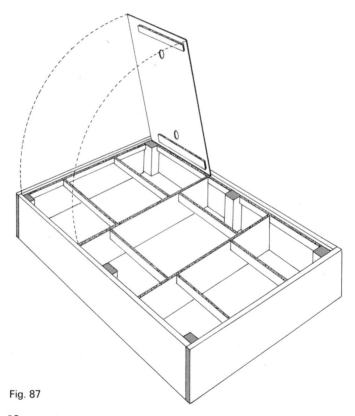

Fig. 87

Headboards

A headboard can be just a veneered sheet, as in fig. 85, or it can be part of a structure designed to incorporate side tables or cabinets as in fig. 101. The timber forming the actual headboard can be any solid sheet of chipboard, plywood or blockboard (lumber core plywood). Changing the bed linen is made much easier if the headboard is attached to the wall, enabling the divan, which is on castors, to be pulled away. If side cabinets are fitted, there must be a gap of three inches between them and the sides of the divan. The headboard in fig. 101 is eight feet wide and stands on two legs hidden by the bed. It is attached to the wall in two places at the back by the method shown in fig. 88, and can very easily be removed by taking out the two nails.

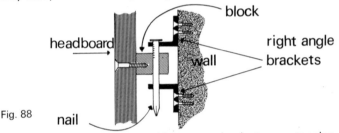

Fig. 88

Since the side cabinets, which were simply two rectangles, had to be capable of bearing a reasonable weight and because they were not supported with legs, a really strong method of fixing them to the headboard was essential. This was done by insetting two 9in. right angle brackets into the headboard and the cabinet tops (fig. 89), in addition to the screws through the headboard into the back of the cabinet edges. With the whole surface veneered they are undetectable.

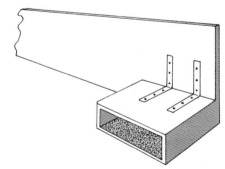

Fig. 89

63

8 Fittings and fixtures

Buy all the fittings before starting on the construction of your furniture. There is nothing more frustrating than discovering, when all the woodwork is completed, that the particular fitting you require is unobtainable or that the way in which the furniture has been constructed inhibits its movement. The following are a few of the more common ones with some notes on how they are fitted.

Door catches

The single ball catch (bullet catch) (fig. 90a) is normally fitted either on the open edge of the door, level with the handle (position a), or, if two are used, in the top and bottom edges (position b). A hole the diameter of the cylinder is drilled in the door edge, and, with the cylinder in place and the door shut, the position of the striking plate can be marked and then screwed to the frame. The double ball catch, (fig. 90b), fitted on the back of the door and the inside of the frame, is designed so that the two halves can come together either face to face or at right angles. (Magnetic or friction catches can also be used but their fitting is more difficult). Again either one or two can be used on each door, but because they are fitted at the back of the door it is easier to mark their positions with the door closed.

Normally I attach the cabinet back only temporarily, so that I can remove it again when fitting the catches.

Fig. 90 a–b

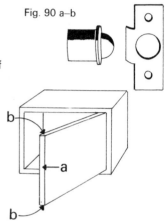

(a) Single ball catch (bullet catch)

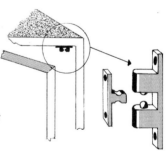

(b) double ball catch

Knobs, handles, pulls and pushes

Knobs and handles are fitted after veneering and their design is a matter of taste. The most important point is the alignment — nothing looks worse than a set of handles which are crooked. For thin sliding doors round pulls can be obtained which are made of coloured plastic. A hole the diameter of the pull is drilled in the door; the pull is then squeezed into it and held either side by double rims. These are used on the cabinet in fig. 53.

Alternatively, you may like to cut your own shapes, backing the pull with $\frac{1}{16}$in. plywood which can be obtained from model-making shops. The shapes are cut by drilling a wide diameter hole in the door, and sawing the shape out with the keyhole saw. If you prefer rounded corners rather than sharp angles these can be made by drilling small diameter holes. Fig. 91 shows a few shapes with the large diameter starting holes, and the smaller corner holes.

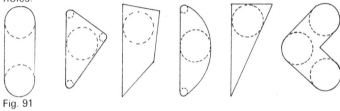

Fig. 91

Instead of handles on lids, as, for example, a gramophone (phonograph) cabinet, finger slots can be cut in the section on which the lid rests (fig. 92a). The easiest way of doing this is to cut out a complete section, the shape of the slot, and reinsert a piece half its thickness as in fig. 92b.

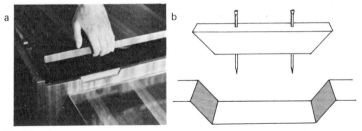

Fig. 92 a–b

Bolts

On wardrobes and cupboards with double doors it is quite common to have one door held by a bolt and the other, the one most frequently opened, held to with single or double ball catches. The type of bolt used is small and flat and is called an extruded cupboard bolt (or cabinet bolt) (fig. 93). The bolts are fitted on the top and bottom of the door, which is then closed to give the position of the striking plates.

Fig. 93

Door stays

If you do not want a door to open beyond a certain angle, you will need a door stay. There is a wide variety available, but the type I find most satisfactory is the one shown in fig. 94a. There are two designs: one with a fixed stay and one where the stay can be unclipped at x. The obvious advantage of the latter is that, should you at any time wish to open the door beyond the stay's limit, you simply have to unclip the arm instead of unscrewing the fitting. The angle to which the door will open is governed by the position of x. In the open position the end of the rod is against x. The further you move fitting x away from z the more you limit

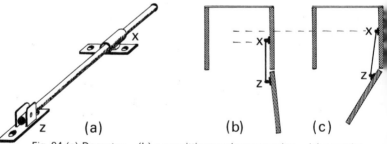

Fig. 94 (a) Door stay (b) x permitting maximum opening (c) x restricting the opening

the opening as shown by figs. 94 b and c. It is best to fit stays at the top of a door, putting z on first, and holding x in various positions until the angle of the opening is as you want it.

Wall attachments

There are numerous ways of attaching items to a wall, but the three I employ most often are glass plates (fig. 95a), keyhole or escutcheon plates (described in chapter 4), and mirror screws (fig. 95b). The uprights in the unit shown on the front cover were attached to the wall with glass plates on their side, positioned so that they would be concealed by the units and the shelves. The cabinets were screwed to the uprights with mirror screws, with a further set of four through their backs into the wall. It is seldom safe to trust the whole weight of a cabinet to mirror screws alone; quite unobtrusive additional support can be given by putting a batten beneath them, as in fig. 95c, which is then veneered to match the rest of the cabinet.

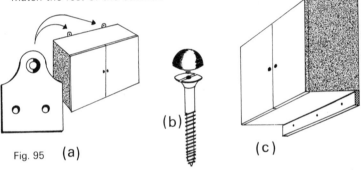

(b)

Fig. 95   (a)   (c)

The shelves illustrated in figs. 69 and 131, make use of the right angles in the walls and both are held sandwiched between battens top and bottom. Both shelves are made from $\frac{3}{4}$in. chipboard, and the one in fig. 69 has a $\frac{1}{2}$in. × 2in. edging board which gives it extra rigidity and the appearance of being thicker.

Ferrules and castors

The best way of protecting the most vulnerable part of veneered furniture, the legs, is to fit something on the bottom, so that the veneer is not touching the floor.

Fig. 96 (a) Glide   (b) ferrule   (c) 'Shepherd' castor

Glides (fig. 96a) which are hammered into the bottom of the leg, adding approximately $\frac{1}{8}$in. to the height, can be used on heavy tables and items of furniture which are seldom moved.

Ferrules, obtainable either square or round, cap the leg, which must be rebated (rabbeted) so that the ferrule and leg retain the same contour. A more elaborate ferrule is available with a fixed or tilted glide, adjustable in height (fig. 96b). This useful combination permits the glide to stand square with the floor, on splayed legs, and it can be slightly adjusted for uneven floors.

For ease of movement, nothing can beat the 'Shepherd' castor, (fig. 96c). This cleverly designed universal wheel will move in any direction and even the smallest can bear considerable weight and still retain their flexibility. They are more expensive than the older type of wheel castor but well worth the additional cost. They are available with various methods of fixing; the type illustrated has a round plate which is screwed to the bottom of the leg or base. When designing furniture, allowance must be made for this height which is upwards of $1\frac{1}{2}$in. Even the heaviest divans and sideboards fitted with 'Shepherd' castors can be moved with one hand.

Hinges

In chapter 6 we examined at some length the fitting of butt hinges; while these are normally used for doors, they are rather unsightly on lids which open on a top surface. The alternative is either a piano hinge (fig. 97), which is one continuous butt hinge and fitted on the same principle, or centre hinges (fig. 98). The latter, which go on the side edges of the lid, are completely hidden when the lid is closed and leave the top surface unbroken.

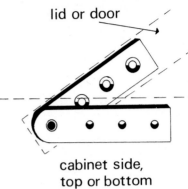

lid or door

cabinet side, top or bottom

Fig. 97 Piano hinge   Fig. 98 Centre hinge

'Ever Ready' drawer

Finally, a little trick which comes under the heading of fittings, but which you can make yourself. It is often useful to have a lift out tray within a drawer (fig. 99) for cutlery, jewelry or pens and

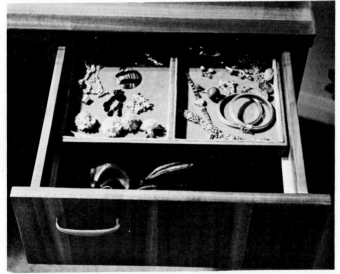

Fig. 99 Jewelry tray in a dressing table

Fig. 100 Dressing table, sapele veneer on blockboard (lumber core plywood)

Fig. 101 Headboard, sapele veneer on chipboard

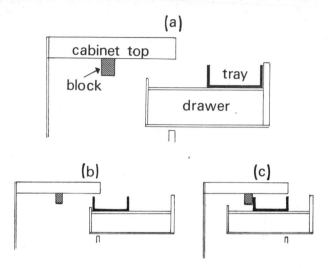

Fig. 102 (a) Drawer open—tray at front   (b) drawer open—tray at back
(c) drawer being closed with block pushing tray to front

pencils, but at the same time one wants the things underneath the tray to be easily accessible without having to lift the tray out. This can be done by putting the tray on runners in the drawer but by also attaching a block above and against the back edge of the tray when the drawer is closed (fig. 102), the tray will always be at the front when the drawer is opened. You will note that the back of the drawer must be lower than the bottom of the block, but high enough to prevent the tray being pushed off.

9 Designing and designs

The outward appearance of your furniture depends very much on your personal taste. You may wish to stick to conventional shapes or build something which is quite unique. Domestic furniture however, must not only be pleasing to look at but also functional.

Usually, bearing in mind the overall size, I find that it is best to think initially in terms of what the item has to do rather than what it will look like. For example, in making a bookcase, instead of deciding that it will be 30in. high and 40in. wide with three shelves, I start by measuring the size of the books and working out the average height and depth of shelf needed to accommodate them. This shows roughly how many shelves I can get within a certain height and on that basis I design the bookcase so that the proportions and general appearance are pleasing. This is a simple example and many others such as the height of tables and the size of drawers will suggest themselves to you.

When designing furniture to take specific items, do not over-look the thickness of the timber. If you decide initially to make a 30in. high bookcase, with a 5in. base and three shelves plus the top of 1 in. thick boards, you will find that there is only 7in. between each shelf—barely enough for an average paperback.

I strongly recommend, therefore, that in designing your furniture, you draw it up to scale showing the thickness of the timber and the positions of the screws and fittings. With a working drawing you can spot the drawbacks and avoid costly errors. It is also a good way of ensuring that only the easily obtainable planed timber sizes are used, that they are cut in the most economical way, and that the right amount is purchased.

Although the furniture we have been looking at is based on the rectangle, the boards forming it do not have to be straight edged nor do they have to be the same width or thickness at each joint. Fig. 103 shows a few ways in which different sizes and shapes can vary the outward appearance whilst retaining the basic rectangle as the starting point. Turn this figure upside down and on its side and see if the diagrams suggest any interesting shapes for your furniture with perhaps legs, top, doors or shelves added.

Other materials combined with wood can produce unusual and attractive results; glass and ceramics lend themselves particularly well to this. The coffee table in fig. 34 has a mosaic top adding a splash of colour and making it easy to keep clean*. Decorative

*Making Mosaics, John Berry, Pocket How To Do It, Studio Vista Limited, London, Watson-Guptill Publications, New York

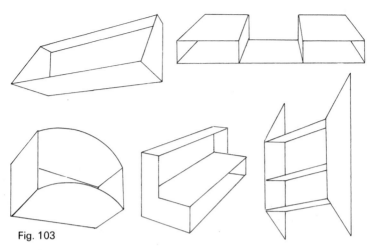

Fig. 103

ceramic tiles would have been equally effective. Quarter inch plate glass with polished edges provides good protection on surfaces which have a lot of wear or are likely to have things spilt on them. It can also be used effectively in place of sliding doors or for shelves, as in the cocktail cabinet in fig. 104.

To conclude this brief section, the following pages of working drawings, showing the sizes of timber, and methods of construction (using the rectangle in a variety of ways) will I hope stimulate your own ideas on design.

Fig. 104

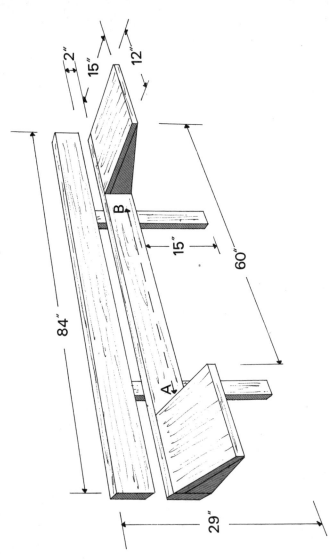

Fig. 105 Headboard. The measurement A-B indicates the position of a 4ft 6in. divan. This measurement can be increased or reduced depending upon the width of the divan but always allow 3in. either side between the divan and side tables. *Materials*—horizontal boards 1in. × 6in.; legs 1in. × 3in. boards; side tables 1in. blockboard.

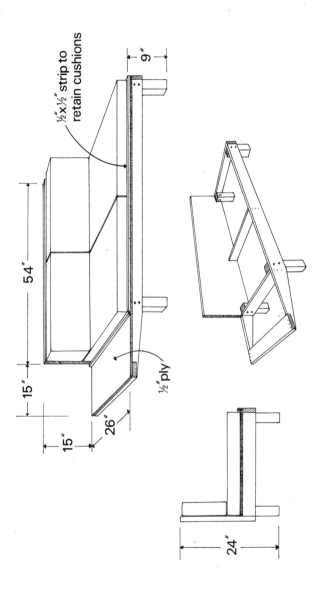

½"×½" strip to retain cushions

9"

54"

15"

½ ply

15"

26"

24"

Fig. 106 Couch and side table. *Materials*—frame 1in. × 3in. boards, back which also forms part of the frame, 1in. blockboard; legs 2in. × 2in. blocks bolted to frame; seat top and side table sheeted with ¼in. plywood, cushion retaining strips ½in. × ½in.; cushions 3in. thick foam rubber.

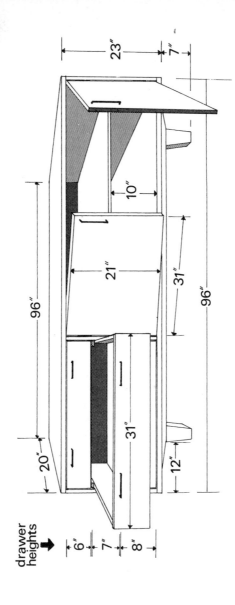

Fig. 107 Sideboard with cupboard and three drawers. *Materials*—external cabinet top, bottom, sides, partition and doors 1in. blockboard; shelves $\frac{1}{2}$in. plywood; cabinet back and drawer bottoms $\frac{1}{4}$in. plywood; drawer frames $\frac{3}{4}$in. boards; runners attached to drawer bottoms $\frac{1}{2}$in. × $\frac{3}{4}$in.; runners attached to cabinet sides $\frac{3}{4}$in. × $\frac{3}{4}$in.; legs 3in. × 2in. blocks; leg battens 1in. × 3in. boards.

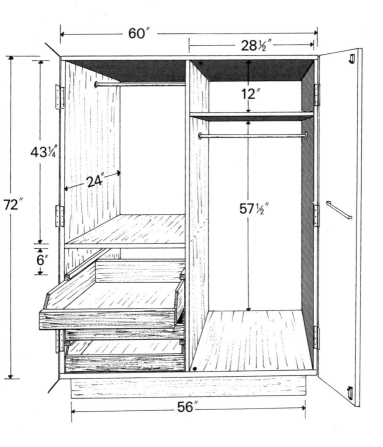

Fig. 108 Wardrobe with full height hanging space for dresses and coats and reduced height for suits and skirts. (Top drawer and left hand door omitted from illustration for clarity.) *Materials*—top, bottom, sides, partition, doors and shelves 1in. blockboard; base and drawers ¾in. boards; wardrobe back and drawer bottoms ¼in. plywood; runners ¾in. × ¾in. strips; hanger rails ¾in. diameter brass tubes.

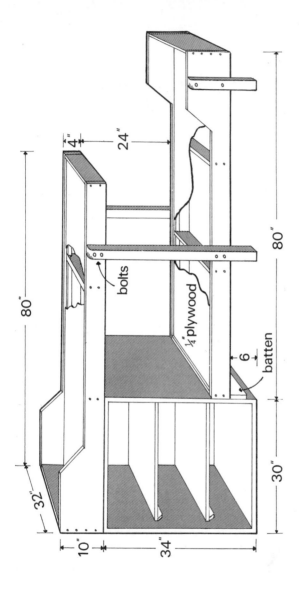

Fig. 109 Bunk beds, 6ft 6in. × 2ft 6in., designed to give full headroom on the lower bunk. *Materials*—bed frames and cupboard frame $\frac{3}{4}$in. blockboard or plywood; bunk tops and cupboard back $\frac{1}{4}$in. plywood; legs 2in. × 2in. $\frac{1}{2}$in. × 1in. strips; bottom bunk batten 1in. × 4in.; two cupboard doors (optional) $\frac{1}{2}$in. plywood. Build each bunk and the cupboard as three separate parts and assemble after veneering.

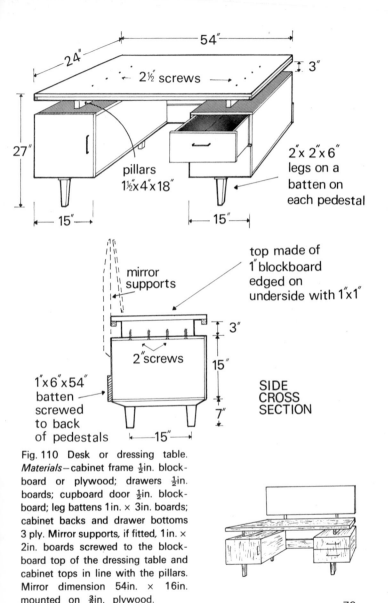

54"

24"

2½" screws

3"

27"

pillars
1½"x4"x18"

2"x 2"x 6"
legs on a
batten on
each pedestal

15"

15"

mirror
supports

top made of
1" blockboard
edged on
underside with 1"x1"

3"

2" screws

15"

1"x 6"x 54"
batten
screwed
to back
of pedestals

15"

7"

SIDE
CROSS
SECTION

Fig. 110 Desk or dressing table.
Materials—cabinet frame ½in. blockboard or plywood; drawers ½in.
boards; cupboard door ½in. blockboard; leg battens 1in. × 3in. boards;
cabinet backs and drawer bottoms
3 ply. Mirror supports, if fitted, 1in. ×
2in. boards screwed to the blockboard top of the dressing table and
cabinet tops in line with the pillars.
Mirror dimension 54in. × 16in.
mounted on ⅜in. plywood.

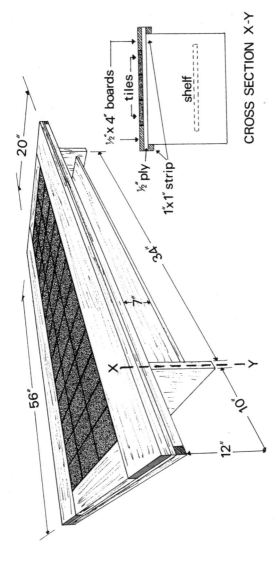

CROSS SECTION X-Y

Fig. 111 Ceramic tiled coffee table with magazine shelf. *Materials*—tile mounting board and shelf ½in. plywood; top surrounds ½in. × 4in. boards; edging strip 1in. × 1in.; legs 1in. × 4in. boards; tiles 4in. × 4in. Complete all woodwork, veneering and finishing, masking the woodwork off before setting the tiles. Use a board laid across the width of the table to ensure that the tops of the tiles are level with the table surround. A sheet of thin plywood or hardboard may be required to raise the bottom of the well, depending upon the thickness of the tiles used.

80

10 Veneers and designing in veneer

I find veneering the most satisfying part of furniture making. As each piece is laid the furniture begins to take on an entirely new appearance and one can picture more clearly how it will look when placed in a room along with other furniture.

Most veneers come from hardwoods, the aristocrats of the forest, and having constructed the furniture from pines and plywoods, which are practically void of any figuring or contrasting grains, it is a welcome change to be working with materials rich in texture and colour.

I would like to dispel at the outset any suggestion that veneering is a means of covering up faulty workmanship. It is a legitimate part of carpentry, and has existed for centuries. It permits a style of design which would be quite impossible to achieve working in solid wood, and, of course, it is far less expensive than solid wood.

A few years ago, veneering was a lengthy process of damping down the leaves (a leaf is a sheet of veneer), heating the glue and clamping the item for several hours while it dried out; now, using impact adhesives (contact cement), each piece can be laid in a matter of minutes and is ready for sanding and finishing as soon as it is down.

Varieties of veneer

There are literally hundreds of different veneers and when the range of figurings, markings and grain effects are also taken into account the number becomes infinite. Suppliers usually keep the leaves in the order they were cut from the tree trunk and store them in batches. Thus leaves from the same batch have almost identical markings and grain effects although, as you work down the batch, the markings alter in shape and some may disappear altogether. In size they vary from two or three to thirty inches across the grain, although in the larger widths they are seldom without blemish. Length is equally variable, ranging from offcuts of a couple of feet up to leaves of sixteen feet.

Much of the best veneer is snapped up by the furniture manufacturers, consequently supplies for the amateur fluctuate a great deal. I have, therefore, considered only the more common varieties, most of which can usually be obtained. They are oak,

Afromosia, teak, sapele, walnut, mahogany and rosewood. In fig. 116, which also includes one example of 'Fineline', a laminated veneer, you will see that in the seven main varieties alone, the colours range from light yellow and golden, through all shades of reddish and pure brown, to almost black. The veneers in fig. 116 were given one application of wax so although they are typical of each species you cannot use them as a colour chart for matching purposes as you would in selecting paint. 'Fineline' is produced in a wide range of attractive, plain or contrasting striped leaves and has two main advantages: its straight grain, and the fact that it can always be matched simply by quoting the manufacturer's reference number.

All timber changes its tone value when given a finish, however transparent. The colours become deeper and richer, and the light and dark areas are thrown into greater contrast. Because of this change in tone, it is useful when selecting leaves to take a damp rag in a polythene bag, to dab them. This will give you a rough guide to the finished shade, although the more finishing applications given, the deeper the tones. It is also worth remembering that oak darkens with age and for this reason it is not advisable to try and match it with timber of a different species, although it can be used for obtaining contrasts.

The grain of veneer, like that of most cut timber, seldom runs parallel with the edges; but it is usually possible, with the seven suggested varieties, to select from batches where it is reasonably straight. To start with, it is best to avoid leaves which are not completely flat or where the grain curves sharply, for whilst this may mean passing over some of the more attractively figured leaves, they may be difficult to cut cleanly.

As you will have realised the types, sizes, colours and grains of veneer can vary so much that you need to find out exactly what is available locally before planning the design. When you visit your local supplier take a tape measure and make a note of the sizes he has in stock. This will help you to avoid wastage.

Designing in veneer

There are two ways to approach the use of veneer. The first is to 'play it straight', relying solely upon the distinctive appearance of the wood to produce a natural design. The second is to treat it as a means of added embellishment and decoration, creating patterns and shapes either by laying matching leaves at different angles or using contrasting colours of veneer. Both methods are equally effective and over large areas a combination of the two can produce very attractive and unusual results. A large wardrobe veneered in alternate light narrow, and darker wide leaves, would not only show off the beauty of the grain in the darker wood but also break up the overall effect of a large dark mass. Sometimes the light and dark effect can be found in the leaf itself, as in the case of the sapele used for the dressing table in fig. 100, and the bed headboard in fig. 101. I was fortunate in discovering a batch of thirty, twelve-foot leaves in which not only was the grain

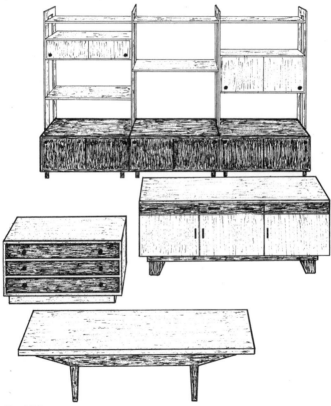

Fig. 112

completely straight, except for the last few inches, but the figuring remained identical throughout. This is not uncommon with sapele and, since it is one of the easiest to cut, it is the ideal veneer to use for your first attempt.

The danger of using veneers of contrasting colour or matching leaves laid at different angles is that it can produce a fussy appearance. The veneer should emphasise the attractive outlines and pleasing proportions of your furniture. The top of a long, low coffee table could be veneered in Afromosia and the 'rectangle' and legs in mahogany. A chest of drawers with frame, top and sides in oak would throw drawers finished in dark rosewood into sharp relief. Walnut used for the cabinets and shelves of a Scandinavian wall unit would add boldness to their outline while the more delicate colouring of oak or Afromosia used for the ladders would heighten their slim elegance. Fig. 112 may give you some ideas on the use of contrasts and the effects that can be achieved; it is helpful to make some sketches such as these when planning what leaves to lay and where. Some veneers con-

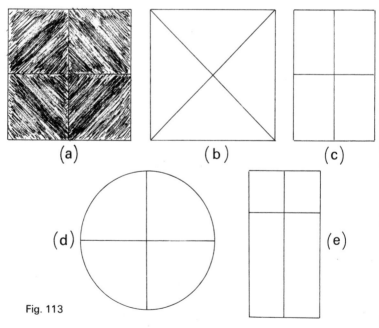

(a) (b) (c)

(d) (e)

Fig. 113

trast well, others are complementary to each other and the choice is a matter of personal taste and, of course, what is available. Generally, I have found it a mistake to use more than two types of veneer on a single item or series of matching items. Sometimes, when using a single, all-over veneer, it is effective just to pick out an inlaid shape behind the handles. It must be a simple shape, such as an oval, a triangle or a crescent and in keeping with both the overall design of the furniture and the shape of the handle or knob.

Fig. 114

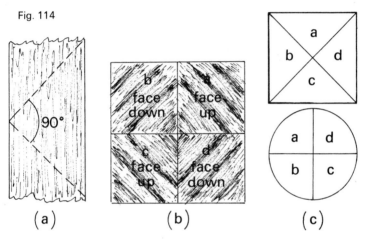

(a)   (b)   (c)

Attractive designs can be produced by laying the leaves at angles to each other (fig. 113a), on one surface only, perhaps a table top, or repeated several times on adjacent doors, or simply run across several surfaces in the same plane, for example the front of a cabinet with drawers. Using this method on the top of furniture, the surface should be divided into equal quarters either from corner to corner or midway along each side (fig. 113b, c, d), but on doors the centre of the design should be roughly at eye level (fig. 113e). The pattern in each of the quadrants must match exactly. This is achieved by selecting four leaves from the same batch which were cut one beneath the other and therefore have identical figuring. Starting from the centre of the design, cut the leaves across the grain in a V shape, with the apex of the V forming a right angle (fig. 114a). Then, as in fig. 114b,

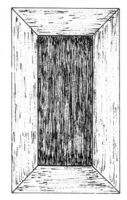

Fig. 115

lay leaves a and c face up diagonally opposite each other and b and d upside down in the other corners. In this way symmetry of design is achieved. Quartering from corner to corner or on a circular surface is done in exactly the same way (fig. 114c) and is ideal for round tables.

You will find that several widths of veneer are needed to cover to the edge of each quadrant and for each width four matching leaves are needed. If you can obtain leaves of sufficient length for all the widths in one quadrant, this is ideal, because the graining effect will then be similar and the colour an exact match. You may find this difficult when quartering several adjacent surfaces in the same pattern, but choose your 'matching fours' from the same batch and use the same area of each leaf in the same place on all the surfaces. Never try and match veneers from different batches for, although you may think you have been successful, when you apply the finish they will probably come up a different shade. An enormous number of patterns and designs can be evolved, to cover the whole or part of the surface. Fig. 115 shows just a few; you will, no doubt, discover many more when thinking in terms of your own furniture.

Although I have described patterns and contrasts at some length I do not wish to imply that this is necessarily preferable to the simplicity of an all-over matched design. The more you work with veneer the more you will appreciate its infinite variety and natural beauty. If you do nothing more than arrange matching leaves side by side, your furniture will acquire a unique distinction.

86

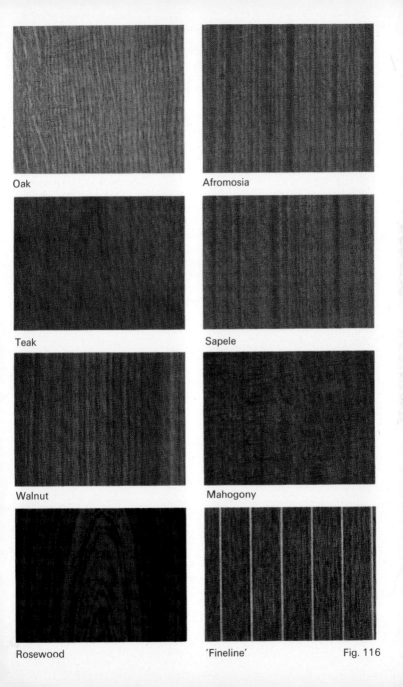

Oak

Afromosia

Teak

Sapele

Walnut

Mahogony

Rosewood

'Fineline'

Fig. 116

Whatever design you decide upon, logic must play an important part in it. The grain should run in a natural direction, creating the impression that the furniture is constructed of solid oak, teak or whatever wood you choose. If you were building a bookcase, the grain would run the length of the shelves and not across them. The same thinking must apply to legs, edges, doors, in fact every piece of veneer you lay. The only time when the rule can be broken is on a suite of furniture where the natural direction is one way on the majority of items but at right angles on a single piece. You will notice that this situation arose with the dressing table (fig. 100), the bed headboard (fig. 101) and the wardrobe which is also part of the suite. On both the wardrobe and headboard the natural direction was vertical but the drawers in the dressing table should, technically, run horizontally. I felt, however, that it would be more effective to maintain the vertical matching design. In the case of the wall unit on the front cover, the same conflict arose with the centre drawer, but here I argued that symmetry was maintained by matching the cabinets vertically on either side and allowing the grain on the drawer to follow the same horizontal direction as the shelves. In some cases it is equally correct for the grain to lay either way, as on the top of a table or cabinet.

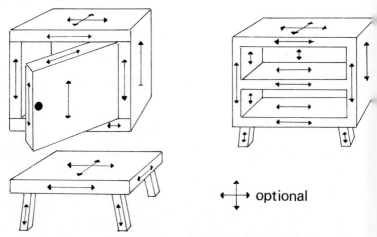

←┼→ optional

Fig. 117 shows some stylized designs with the edges thickened for the purpose of illustration; the arrows indicate the direction in which the grain would normally run.

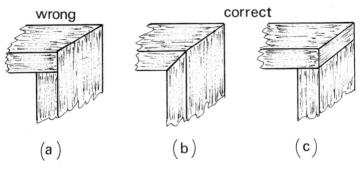

wrong

correct

(a)   (b)   (c)

Fig. 118

The second point of logic to bear in mind concerns the corners and adjacent surfaces. If you look at fig. 118a, you will see that, face on, the timber has been butt jointed, but along the top surface and side it appears to be mitred. Either b or c would be correct; b shows the mitre on the face as well as the top and side; c continues the butt joint on the side surface. I prefer to use b because with veneer it is not possible to simulate the end grain effect which c should, technically, have. Fig. 119a shows another 'howler'. Obviously, if the grain runs the length of the timber on the top surface it must do the same along the thickness.

Finally, on the subject of design, let us consider the shape of surfaces. Across the grain, veneer will bend or roll to a relatively small diameter, in many species down to about one inch, which makes it quite easy to veneer small rounded legs. With the grain however, I have found two feet to be about the smallest safe diameter without the risk of cracking. Leaves vary in flexibility depending upon their thickness, texture and the regularity of the grain. If they become too dry they will be brittle and liable to split in either direction although, as I will explain in the chapter on laying veneer, there are ways of minimizing this risk.

wrong   correct

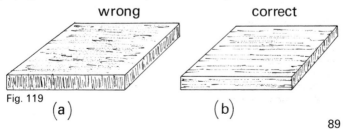

Fig. 119
(a)   (b)

Planning your requirements

By far the easiest way of working out what area of veneer you will require is to use graph paper, ruled in $\frac{1}{12}$th squares, each square representing an inch. The size of the leaves and all the surfaces to be covered can then be drawn to scale. This helps in positioning the prominent surfaces on the most attractive areas of the leaf and helps to avoid awkward sized offcuts.

If you are planning several matching pieces of furniture, it is essential to buy all the veneer for the main surfaces at the same time, even if it means storing it for several months while you construct the various items. It is, however, quite normal to use a cheaper veneer of the same wood but different grain for the surfaces which are less noticeable, such as the underneath of shelves or the insides of cabinets and drawers. Prices depend very much on the quality and figuring of the leaves.

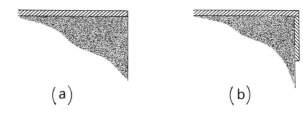

Fig. 120

For each surface you will need to allow between $\frac{1}{4}$in. and $\frac{1}{2}$in. on all sides for trimming. Although it is not necessary to cover backs or undersides which will be hidden, finishing any surface at an edge, as in fig. 120a, is not very satisfactory because it is liable to catch in clothing or dusters. A better method is to add a 1in. 'turnover' strip, as in fig. 120b.

Having bought your leaves, lay them out side by side in the order in which they were cut, exactly aligning the figuring. Then mark them out as planned. I find it advisable to number all the pieces making up each surface before they are cut, otherwise it is only too easy to lay a piece the wrong way up or back to front, thereby losing the symmetry.

11 Laying veneer

Tools and equipment

The tools which you will require for veneering were mentioned in chapter 1 and are: the trimming knife, steel rule, smooth plane, and G cramps (C clamps). A comb for spreading the impact adhesive (contact cement) is normally supplied with the adhesive itself but, if it is not, a piece of formica or masonite, 2in. × 4in. with

straight, bevelled edges will do equally well. You will however need two essential 'aids'. The first is a smoothing block—a strip of ½in. × 2in. hardwood about 6in. long. At one end this needs to be round-edged, as shown in fig. 121, and to make it run freely on the veneer, the rounded edge can be polished by rubbing it up and down on another piece of hardwood.

Fig. 121

The smoothing block is used to 'iron' the veneer flat, getting rid of any air bubbles. The second aid is a planing clamp. This is used for holding one or more leaves while the edges are planed straight for butt jointing (fig. 122). Although you will not often want to use the full length, it is useful to make it at least seven feet long so that leaves suitable for 6ft 6in. doors can be prepared. The materials you require are one 7ft hardwood board ½in. × 5in., two 7ft hardwood boards 1in. × 4in., both of which must have absolutely straight edges, and a 30in. block of 1½in. × 1½in. softwood. Screw one of the 1in. × 4in. boards to the wider board down the whole of its length, leaving a 1in. platform on the wider board. Place the second narrow board exactly over the first and hold it in position with a coach (carriage) bolt and wing nut at each end. It is very important to get the leading edges of the narrower boards flush with each other because these surfaces govern the accuracy of the plane. Cut the softwood block into six 5in. lengths and screw these to the base to form a series of equally spaced feet.

Almost any number of leaves can be held at one time in the planing clamp, each protruding sufficiently to clear any nicks or

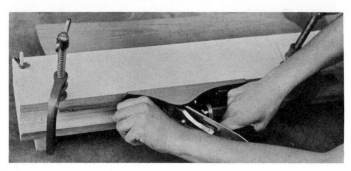

Fig. 122

splinters along their edges. Lay the smooth plane on its side on the wider board at right angles to the protruding leaves. Then, taking care not to push too hard against them, gently plane the leaves down to the edges of the narrower boards. To hold the boards tightly together, I find it best to use at least three G cramps (C clamps), upside down, along the length of the planing clamp, trimming the section between each and moving one cramp at a time to avoid upsetting the alignment of the leaves. One must also take care not to plane into the leading edges of the narrower boards which hold the leaves as this will render the clamp inaccurate. Trimming separate leaves, either across or with the grain, is done with the knife against the steel rule, drawing the blade across the surface several times, the weight of the knife doing most of the work. Trim one leaf at a time, cutting on a smooth surface — hardboard is ideal. If the knife tends to follow the grain rather than the edge of the rule, damp the leaf down and it will cut easily, but remember to allow time for it to dry before putting on the adhesive.

Preparing the surfaces·

All the surfaces to be veneered must be completely free of dust and perfectly level. A good test is to run the back of the square blade across them. If it rocks or catches anywhere, then you know you have more preparation to do. Hairline cracks and tiny pit marks do not matter, but screw heads which are not flush with the surface will need to be filled. The best filler is the sort used for cracks in wall plaster because it can be sanded level when dry and does not shrink. Joins in the timber are particularly important, they must be flush and either planed or filed wherever there is the slightest unevenness.

Laying flat leaves

In the early stages I would advise you to allow $\frac{1}{4}$in. to $\frac{1}{2}$in. overlap for trimming round the edge of the surfaces. This is because of the nature of impact adhesive (contact cement). Once it is down it cannot be moved even a fraction of an inch, consequently it is best to leave a little margin, in case, in the laying, long leaves get slightly out of alignment. With practice you will be able to reduce this margin to as little as $\frac{1}{8}$in. and, in some cases, lay it completely flush with the edge of the surface.

Impact adhesives (contact cements), vary slightly from make to make; in most cases you will need to apply a thin even layer, with a comb, to both surfaces. They are left for fifteen to twenty minutes until the adhesive is completely dry to touch and then both surfaces are laid together, the bond being instantaneous.

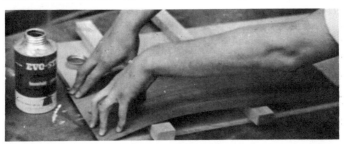

Fig. 123

There are two methods of laying leaves, each aimed at keeping the coated surfaces apart while they are positioned, and I would suggest you experiment with both to find out which method you prefer. The first way is to lay a number of 1in. × 1in. blocks (fig. 123), slightly longer than the width of the leaf, at 6in. to 8in. intervals along the coated surface, laying the leaf on top of these. Starting at one end, press the tip of the leaf onto the edge of the surface so that it just makes contact, then, providing the alignment is correct, remove the blocks one by one while the leaf is pressed down. The second method uses a sheet of brown paper instead of the blocks. Slide the paper out gradually and press the two surfaces together (fig. 124). Whichever method you use the most important point is to make the initial contact on the narrowest possible area, about $\frac{1}{16}$in., i.e. just sufficient for it to anchor while you check the alignment down the length of the leaf. With small narrow strips of veneer you will probably find that you are able to hold the strip away from the surface with one hand, using the other to manipulate it.

Fig. 124

Once the leaf is laid, go over the whole area with the smoothing block, starting from the centre and working up and down the grain, out towards the sides. Use firm pressure and work over the whole surface until the adhesive ceases to crackle. Take great care to obtain a really good bond at the edges. Another way of testing the bond is to tap the surface with your finger nail. If it sounds like paper, more smoothing is needed.

On wide, flat surfaces the leaves will require invisible butt jointing. First ensure that the edges of the leaf are absolutely straight by using the planing clamp. There are then two ways of dealing with the butt joints. The first is to lay each leaf separately, holding it between the fingers of both hands, and pressing its edge against the edge of the leaf already laid (fig. 125). With this method, ignore what might be happening to the other side of the leaf. Although it is probably very uneven, it will lie flat when the smoothing block is used. The alternative method is to join all the leaves together with masking tape on the top surfaces before laying them and then to put them down as one piece. Although this means working with a large area of veneer it is much easier for patterned designs. With inlaid work, setting contrasting grains or colours within larger leaves, both pieces *must* be cut out over each other and the taping method of butt jointing used.

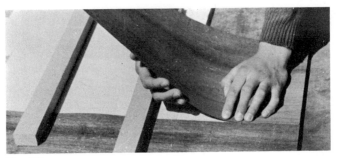

Fig. 125

Trimming

The way in which the waste is trimmed depends on the direction of the grain. Across the grain, the veneer can be trimmed flush and the waste removed in one piece. Draw a faint line on the top surface of the veneer to mark the position of the cut, and place the steel rule against it. Using the knife at right angles to the leaf, with a sawing movement, cut towards you on the downward stroke only. The waste will come away in a curl and, if the knife is sharp, you will be left with a clean flush edge (fig. 126). With the grain, you must always cut in the direction in which the grain runs off the leaf. Never attempt to trim flush to the edge with the first cut and do not try to remove a piece of waste the whole length of the leaf because the knife can veer inwards and may draw a splinter from the veneered surface. Always start with a line on the top of the leaf to mark the edge of the surface then take a series of slithers (fig. 127) working back towards the line and finishing off

Fig. 126

Fig. 127

with a flourpaper (garnet paper) block held at right angles to the edge; but take care not to round the edge. If you keep the edge square, you will find that when you make the edge joint at right angles, the two surfaces merge to give the appearance of solid wood. Corners are extremely vulnerable and need just enough sanding to make them smooth. By *over* perfecting, you will rub down to the surface on which the veneer is laid and once this happens there is nothing you can do to cover it up.

Order of laying leaves

To give the maximum protection to the edges, the leaves should nearly always be laid so that horizontal surfaces overlap vertical ones (fig. 128a). Then, if heavy or rough articles are slid across a top there is no danger of pulling the edge away. The same rule applies to legs which will almost certainly be dragged across floors and rough carpets. With drawers, however, the rule should be reversed, and

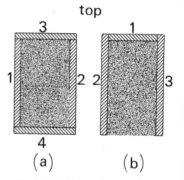

Fig. 128 (a) legs, shelves, sides, edges (b) drawers

the strip covering the thickness set between the vertical surfaces of the sides and front, as items are usually lifted out of a drawer (fig. 128b).

Rounded surfaces

There are two ways to tackle cylindrical surfaces, such as rounded legs. The first is to roll the leg in a sheet of brown paper, mark the point where the two surfaces overlap, cut a template and then cut

96

the veneer to the same shape. Generally I find it easier and quicker to cut the leaf a little wider than the circumference of the leg, apply the adhesive and roll the leg onto the veneer, sanding away the portion which overlaps. The resulting butt joint is undetectable. As mentioned in the previous chapter, the grain should run down the leg.

Internal surfaces

The drawback of leaving the internal surfaces until all the construction has been completed is that, first, each section of veneer has to be cut exactly to size and placed very accurately in position, and, second, it is extremely difficult to rub into right angle corners and get them completely smooth. Although it means clearing a space on the bench for the veneer at a time when you would far rather be getting on with the construction, it will always save you time in the long run, and produce a much better result, if you veneer the insides of all items before any of the separate components are screwed together.

First aid

It must appear in this chapter on laying veneer that there are far more 'don'ts' than 'dos' The fact is that laying a leaf of veneer is extremely easy and can be done relatively quickly, but the secret of successful veneering lies in the way it is trimmed and finished, and the extra time taken over this will be repaid not only in the appearance but also in the durability of the finished item. Always take special care over the edges, making sure that a really firm bond is achieved, because it is here that lifting can start, and once the edge lifts it is only a matter of time before a splinter comes away.

Although you will soon discover what can be easily and quickly done and what takes a little longer, there are one or two things which can go wrong and these may discourage not only the beginner but the experienced workman. Mishaps, however, are seldom disastrous.

The most common one is a leaf of veneer splitting along the grain, sometimes the whole of its length. The remedy is adhesive tape or masking tape. Push the two pieces together, making sure no splinters are lost, and tape the leaf every few inches across the width, on the top side. Once the leaf is down the tape can be peeled off and the crack will be quite invisible. Another fairly common mishap is a splinter coming away on the edge of a surface. This can very easily happen when trimming with the grain. If you have the splinter simply coat it and the surface with adhesive and put it back, going over it with the smoothing block. If the splinter is missing select a matching chip of veneer and use this instead. As it is likely that the end of the missing splinter will have snapped, leaving a jagged break, break the edge of the replacement and push the two jagged breaks into each other (fig. 129).

Your butt joints may cause a problem by having a hairline (or wider) gap. As with the splinter, find or cut a slither slightly wider than the gap, coat both in adhesive and press the two together, sanding off with flourpaper (garnet paper) until the surface is completely level. If, after the veneer has been down several months, a slight bubble occurs, providing the surface will not be damaged with rubbing, it can be pricked with a pin and then pressed flat with the smoothing block. Alternatively you can lay a wide flat board over the bubble and bang it down with the mallet.

Earlier in this chapter I said that when two surfaces were brought together with impact adhesive they could never be parted. This is true, but if a piece of veneer does have to be stripped off in an emergency, it can be done with a chisel. Take care, however, not to damage the under surface or the edges of the leaves on either side. It is not easy, it takes a long time and of course you will then have to fit the replacement leaf very carefully, but better that than a surface which disappoints you every time you see it.

12 The finish

The type of finish you decide upon is largely a matter of taste and can range from matt to high gloss, but, whichever you choose, the preparation is most important, for whilst the finish will bring out the grain it will also highlight the blemishes. All the surfaces, edges and corners must be critically examined from every angle, cracks filled and areas which feel slightly uneven gone over with the smoothing block.

Fig. 130

The best filler is a mixture of glue and fine sawdust of the same wood, and I find it useful to sweep all the clean sawdust into a tin for this purpose. Mix it up as required and spread it with your finger, then, when dry, rub down, if necessary applying another layer. The rubbing down should be done with flourpaper or 00 gauge glasspaper (sandpaper). Always rub with the grain in order to avoid deep scratches as it is almost impossible to get rid of these without rubbing a hole in the leaf. Again great care must be exercised along the edges. Two or three light sweeps with the flourpaper bent at right angles held between the thumb and forefinger should be quite sufficient (fig. 130). The pressure needs to be on the surfaces forming the edge *not* on the edge itself. Also, avoid drawing the flourpaper across a corner.

You may notice that the impact adhesive has got onto some of the visible surfaces. Although it may not be very apparent at this stage, it will become far more so as soon as any finish is applied. Small areas can be rubbed off with flourpaper or your finger but more persistent patches require the special adhesive thinners. Use this with caution. As it is a solvent it will quickly seep through the veneer and cause lifting. A little on a rag will soften the adhesive and continued rubbing with the rag wrapped round your finger should remove it. A knife blade drawn across the surface at an angle of about 75° may also help. As with all remedial operations prevention is better than cure.

Staining

Having taken the trouble to select veneers of pleasing colours it seems a pity to alter their shades with stain, but this is sometimes necessary if you wish to make a match with an existing piece of furniture. Of the three types of stain, spirit, water and oil, spirit is the easiest to use as it does not raise the grain. It can be obtained ready mixed or in a variety of coloured powders to which methylated spirit is added. Mix sufficient to give one coat to an entire piece of furniture and build up to the required colour through several very diluted applications. Work quickly, using a camel hair brush, starting at one edge and sweeping the length of the grain. This way you will only have one wet edge and can avoid putting on a double density by going over the same area twice. Allow each coat to dry before applying the next and bear in mind that the finish on top of this will add further depth to the tone. With all finishes it is best to experiment on a piece of scrap wood and this is particularly necessary when staining.

Matt finish

Most modern furniture is left in its natural colour and given either a matt or sheen finish rather than a high gloss. This type of finish is easy to apply and has two great advantages—it is durable and easily renovated.

Teak oil (or boiled linseed oil), which gives a matt or semi-sheen finish, can be applied to all veneers. The first coat should be put on with a swab or rag, the surplus wiped off, and allowed to dry for twenty-four hours. With the second and third thinner coats the surfaces should be lightly rubbed down while they are wet and the excess wiped off with a dry rag. A fourth, very light coat will produce a sheen which can either be left as it is or very lightly rubbed down with flourpaper. A wipe over from time to time with a rag dipped in teak or other finishing oil and wrung out will maintain this finish.

Sheen finish

Either domestic wax furniture polish or beeswax provides a good finish. Beeswax should be sliced, mixed with turpentine or white spirit and melted in a tin on a hot plate. Take care not to get it near a naked flame. When it is cold, it should be like soft butter and applied evenly with a swab or hardish brush. Leave the wax to set hard in a cool, dry atmosphere for twenty-four hours and then polish it up with a mutton cloth or a similar soft cloth. The more applications, the deeper the sheen, but as maintenance requires further applications of wax, the surface eventually builds up rather unevenly and it is necessary to strip it down with a solution of warm water and vinegar and start again.

Fig. 131
Gloss finish

For a very high gloss finish, polyurethane, which is both a sealer and a glaze, can be used. The first coat is applied sparingly with a clean cloth in parallel strokes and allowed to dry for about four hours. After a light sanding, further coats can be added with a brush. The more coats, the greater the gloss.

My aim in this book has been to demonstrate the ease with which domestic furniture can be made. Perhaps the wardrobe and dressing alcove in fig. 132, which is built up, not by the rectangle principle, but piece by piece on the wall, and finished in contrasting mahogany veneer and magnolia paint may suggest many new and exciting ways of extending your hobby.

For further reading

A B C of Furniture Making by John and Rosemary Christopher, Faber and Faber, 25s

The Complete Book of Woodwork by Charles H. Hayward, Evans Brothers Ltd., 30s

Modern Furniture by Ella Moody, Dutton Vista Pictureback, 10s 6d, $1.95

How to make Built-in Furniture by Mario Dal Fabro, John Murray, 42s, McGraw Hill, $6.95

You should also look in magazines for additional design ideas. Particularly rich sources are: *Interiors* and *Interior Design* in America; *Design* in Great Britain; and *Domus* in Italy (has an English text). *Decorative Art,* an annual edited by Ella Moody, is also an excellent source (Studio Vista, London and The Viking Press, New York).

List of suppliers (UK)

The Art Veneers Co. Ltd, 20 Station Estate, South Woodford, London E 18 specializes in mail order veneer supplies. 112 page catalogue available at 2s 6d, 15 specimens supplied for 1s extra.

Stanley Works (G.B.) Ltd, Woodside, Sheffield 3. Tools distributed through retail shops.
Your local classified telephone directory will have details of timber merchants.

List of suppliers (USA)

Stanley Hand and Power tools are generally available in hardware stores and retail shops throughout the United States. The company will send a catalogue free. The Stanley Works, Hand and Power Tools Division, 600 Myrtle St, New Britain, Conn.

The firm Constantine and Sons, 2040 Eastchester Rd, Bronx. N.Y. 10461 is a mail order business specializing exclusively in materials for veneering. Catalogue upon request and receipt of 25¢. Ask them to enclose their booklet *Veneering Made Easy.*

'Fineline' laminated veneer is available in the USA from William L. Marshall, Ltd, 450 Park Ave. South, New York, N.Y. 10016. Direct your inquiries or requests to Mr George Kinley.

Consult the Yellow Pages of your local telephone directory for lumber yards in your area.

Index